KIDS
ON THE
MARCH

KIDS ON THE MARCH

15 STORIES OF SPEAKING OUT, PROTESTING, AND FIGHTING FOR JUSTICE

MICHAEL G. LONG

Algonquin Young Readers 2021

To all the courageous young people who have marched for a better world

Published by Algonquin Young Readers
an imprint of Algonquin Books of Chapel Hill
Post Office Box 2225
Chapel Hill, North Carolina 27515-2225

a division of Workman Publishing
225 Varick Street
New York, New York 10014

LIBRARY OF CONGRESS CATALOGING-IN-PUBLICATION DATA
Names: Long, Michael G., author.
Title: Kids on the march : 15 stories of speaking out, protesting, and fighting for
    justice / Michael G. Long.
Other titles: 15 stories of speaking out, protesting, and fighting for justice
Description: First edition. | Chapel Hill, North Carolina : Algonquin Young Readers, 2021.
    | Includes bibliographical references. | Audience: Ages 9–12 | Audience: Grades 4–6 |
    Summary: "Kids have always been on the front lines of the fights for justice. From marches
    protesting child labor to the student strike that helped build the case for Brown v. Board of
    Education to modern-day March for Our Lives and the Climate Strike, 'Kids on the March'
    tells the empowering story of children and teens throughout the twentieth and early twenty-
    first century rallying to fight for liberty, justice, and equality"—Provided by publisher.
Identifiers: LCCN 2020044375 | ISBN 9781643751009 (hardcover) | SBN 9781643751665 (ebook)
Subjects: LCSH: Children—Political activity—United States—History—Juvenile literature.
    | Teenagers—Political activity—United States—History—Juvenile literature. | Civil rights
    movements—United States—History—Juvenile literature. | Social action—United States—
    History—Juvenile literature.
Classification: LCC HQ784.P5 L66 2021 | DDC 320.083/0973—dc23
LC record available at https://lccn.loc.gov/2020044375

10 9 8 7 6 5 4 3 2 1
First Edition

*Let us pray with our legs. Let us march in unison
to the rhythm of justice, because I say enough is enough.*

Demetri Hoth
Senior at Marjory Stoneman Douglas High School
2018

Kids on the March

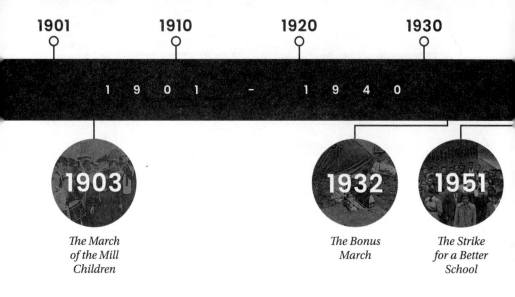

1901   1910   1920   1930

1 9 0 1 — 1 9 4 0

1903

The March
of the Mill
Children

1932

The Bonus
March

1951

The Strike
for a Better
School

Introduction
Kids on the March

"Today, we march, we fight, we *roar!*"

Delaney Tarr, a student at Marjory Stoneman Douglas High School in Parkland, Florida, spoke those powerful words at the student-led March for Our Lives in Washington, DC, on March 24, 2018.

She'd been "freaking out" just before her speech, but as she stood at the podium on the main stage, thousands of marchers saw a poised, confident, and determined young woman.

"We know what we want, we know how to get it, and we are not waiting any longer!" she declared. The crowd thundered its support.

Many of the marchers on that chilly spring day were elementary, middle, and high school students from across the country. Called together by the Parkland students, they had

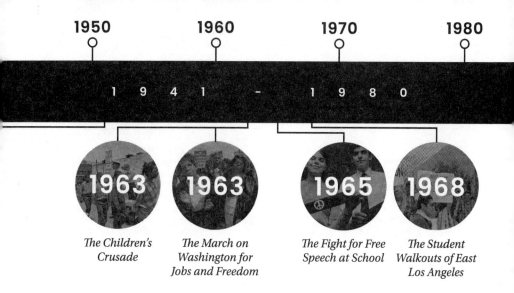

1963

The Children's Crusade

1963

The March on Washington for Jobs and Freedom

1965

The Fight for Free Speech at School

1968

The Student Walkouts of East Los Angeles

gathered at the nation's capital to protest for gun control legislation that would help prevent the type of mass shooting that had occurred at Stoneman Douglas just a month earlier.

As Tarr continued her speech, countless kids raised their protest signs high: WHAT DO YOU LIKE MORE, GUNS OR KIDS?; PROTEST GUNS, NOT KIDS; and #ENOUGH IS ENOUGH!

A short while later, Yolanda Renee King, the nine-year-old granddaughter of Martin Luther King Jr. and Coretta Scott King, also spoke. She said, "I have a dream that enough is enough and that this world should be a gun-free world, period!"

Marchers who had studied her grandfather in history class probably recognized that her words echoed Dr. King's most famous speech, "I Have a Dream," which he gave at the March on Washington for Jobs and Freedom on August 28, 1963. That day about 250,000 protesters demanded an end to racial segregation in businesses, schools, and workplaces.

When we think of protests in US history, we often call to mind Dr. King and his adult colleagues marching together for racial justice in the civil rights movement.

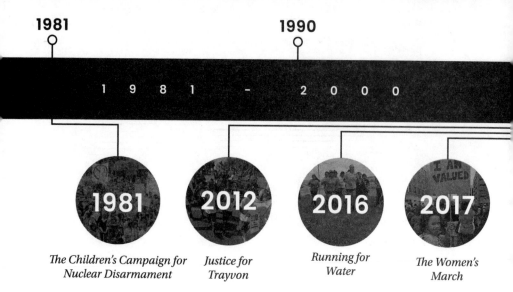

1981
1990

1 9 8 1 — 2 0 0 0

1981
The Children's Campaign for Nuclear Disarmament

2012
Justice for Trayvon

2016
Running for Water

2017
The Women's March

But did you know that many participants in the 1963 March on Washington were kids? Did you know, too, that several months before the March on Washington, thousands of young Black people marched against racial segregation in Birmingham, Alabama? Did you know that this was not the first time in US history that kids marched for justice?

Sixty years earlier, in 1903, child laborers marched from Philadelphia to New York to protest the dangerous working conditions in textile mills.

Even this early march was not the first of its kind.

Young people have led or participated in numerous marches throughout the twentieth and twenty-first centuries. Kids did not always play a leading role. They were mostly behind the scenes in the 1932 Bonus Army March, for example, but sometimes kids were *the* main organizers, the movers and shakers, as the Parkland kids were at the March for Our Lives.

Whether they led or followed, the kids in these historic marches were tough, bold, and brave. Some of these marches

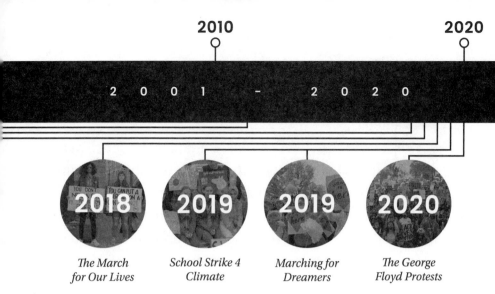

2010

2020

2 0 0 1 — 2 0 2 0

2018

2019

2019

2020

*The March
for Our Lives*

*School Strike 4
Climate*

*Marching for
Dreamers*

*The George
Floyd Protests*

occurred in the face of violence, and others in relative safety, but all of them required courage.

When the Birmingham kids marched, local police officers turned their German shepherds on them. Firefighters blasted them with water from high-pressure hoses. But the kids marched on, demonstrating remarkable bravery in the face of life-threatening danger.

Other protests, like the March for Our Lives, occurred in peaceful settings, but even these commanded bravery. When Stoneman Douglas student Carly Novell prepared to march that day, she feared there would be gun violence. Still, she marched.

Unfortunately, courage has not always translated into success. Some marches succeeded in persuading legislators and the public, others failed, and still others set the stage for change farther down the road of history.

After President John F. Kennedy saw Birmingham police officers attacking the young marchers, he went on national television to denounce racial segregation and propose new legislation to help advance civil rights—exactly what the young people wanted.

In Florida, the March for Our Lives ultimately failed to persuade President Donald J. Trump to back new bills for gun control. Still, the march resulted in legislative success in several states, and it laid groundwork for future federal action.

Despite differences in style, settings, and success rates, the marches in which kids have participated are all deeply connected. They have sought to establish peace, justice, and freedom for all. Each has attempted to fulfill the civil rights identified in the US Constitution. Each has tried to hold the nation accountable to the beliefs and principles set forth in the Declaration of Independence.

As leaders and participants, kids have fought on the front lines of virtually every important march for first-class citizenship throughout US history. When democracy was threatened, kids were there. When people on the margins needed a voice of protest, kids were there. In some cases, kids were there, marching and chanting, long before adults even thought about protesting.

You, too, can march. If you don't like a law that causes suffering, or if you would like a new policy that could help create a better world, you, like the kids in this book, can stand up. You can straighten your shoulders. You can throw back your chin. And you can shout what young people have been shouting for decades: "Let's march!"

Author's note: Kids have participated in many more protests than those highlighted in this book. They've been on the front line in fights for LGBTQ+ rights, disability rights, and animal rights, just to name a few. As you read the pages ahead, think of other protests that you can add to the history of kids on the march. O

PART ONE

The Twentieth Century

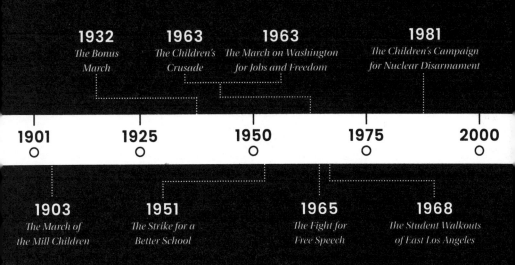

1932
*The Bonus
March*

1963
*The Children's
Crusade*

1963
*The March on Washington
for Jobs and Freedom*

1981
*The Children's Campaign
for Nuclear Disarmament*

1901   **1925**   **1950**   **1975**   **2000**

1903
*The March of
the Mill Children*

1951
*The Strike for a
Better School*

1965
*The Fight for
Free Speech*

1968
*The Student Walkouts
of East Los Angeles*

CHAPTER ONE

The March of the Mill Children

1903

*Mother Jones leads
her "textile army"*

1901   1905   1910

WE ONLY ASK FOR JUSTICE

WE WANT TO GO TO SCHOOL

MORE TIME TO EAT OUR MEALS

These were just three of the messages that children, some as young as ten years old, carried on banners as they silently marched through the streets of Philadelphia on June 17, 1903. They were protesting the unsafe working conditions in factories that produced yarns, threads, and fabrics. They were also demanding a workweek of fifty-five rather than sixty hours, even if it meant cutting their already low wages.

Textile factories were dangerous places. The dusty air was filled with tiny silk threads that caused the children who worked there to cough and wheeze. The piercing sounds of the whirring machines also damaged their hearing. If they accidentally touched the machines in the wrong place, they lost fingers and even hands.

The workweek felt like forever. Children in textile factories labored at least ten hours a day for six days a week. Meanwhile, kids from families with more money went to school, played at recess, and enjoyed lunches and long breaks. By the end of each day, the factory children were exhausted and hungry. Their tired and worn bodies began to bend toward the ground.

It was Mother Jones who planned the march from Independence Hall to City Hall on June 17, 1903.

The children's silent march was a way to help the general public, and especially political leaders, understand the horrible circumstances of their working lives.

As the young workers marched away from Independence Hall, where our nation's Founding Fathers had adopted the Declaration of Independence and the US Constitution, they carried small American flags, symbols of a nation that praised freedom and justice for all. They ended their patriotic march at City Hall, in the center of downtown, where a large crowd of supporters had gathered to hear a famous speaker known as Mother Jones.

Mary Harris—that was the real name of Mother Jones—traveled the country, delivering fiery speeches and helping to organize coal miners and railroad and factory workers. She received her nickname from the grateful union members. Jones's passion for justice was motivated by the tragedies that marked her life. Her husband, George, and four children all died in 1867 during an epidemic of yellow fever. "All around my house I could hear weeping and the cries of delirium," she said years later. "All day long, all night long,

Child laborers at a textile mill in Fall River, Massachusetts, in 1912.

I heard the grating of the wheels of the death cart," a horse-drawn carriage that carried victims of the fever. She also noticed that most of the people suffering from the fever were from poor households. "The rich and the well-to-do fled the city."

After that, Jones moved to Chicago, where she opened a dressmaking business frequented by wealthy women and their families. It pained her to see all the impoverished people outside her shop. "I would look out of the plate glass windows and see the poor, shivering wretches, jobless and hungry, walking along the frozen lake front," she said. Jones experienced yet another tragedy when the Great Chicago Fire of 1871 destroyed her business and everything she owned. With nothing left, she joined the ranks of the poor and destitute. But

Mother Jones and spectators before the start of the March of the Mill Children in Philadelphia.

rather than despairing, she became active in the labor movement and its efforts to help everyday workers improve their living and working conditions.

It was Mother Jones who planned the march from Independence Hall to City Hall in 1903. She had arrived in Philadelphia just a few months earlier to help coordinate a strike. About one hundred thousand textile workers were demanding a reduction of hours in their workweek. Soon after arriving, she was shocked to

It was time for the city to admit that its mansions "were built on the broken bones, the quivering hearts and drooping heads of these children."

learn that about sixteen thousand of the strikers were children from poor families.

These children worked in the factories because their families couldn't afford food and shelter without that money. Pennsylvania laws prohibited children under the age of thirteen from working, but some parents were so desperate that they lied about their kids' ages.

Mother Jones was surprised not only by the number of child workers but also by their appearance. As she recalled, "Every day little children came into union headquarters, some with their hands off, some with the thumb missing, some with their fingers off at the knuckle. They were stooped little things, round shouldered and skinny."

Deeply affected by the suffering, Jones organized the silent march of the children and agreed to speak at the rally at City Hall. The crowd cheered as she climbed atop a table on the steps of the majestic government building. Two small boys joined her, and she gently touched their heads as she began to speak. "One of these boys has had his tongue taken out by the machinery;

On July 15, Mother Jones announced a dramatic change in plans . . .

the other has had his hand almost severed in the mills." It was time for the city to admit that its mansions "were built on the broken bones, the quivering hearts and drooping heads of these children."

The march did not accomplish a reduction in work hours, and Mother Jones thought about next steps that she and the children might take to advance their cause. Then she read that the Liberty Bell was being taken on a tour across the country, and she had an idea. Mother Jones proposed that she and the children go on a tour to draw the nation's attention to the injustices of child labor.

She asked the parents of working children if they would allow their sons and daughters to join her for a march from Philadelphia to New York City, which was home to many bankers and factory owners. These wealthy businesspeople could influence politicians to pass laws that would improve the children's lives. The ninety-two-mile march would last about ten days, and she promised to take care of the children and keep them safe. Many of the parents agreed, and some even joined the protest.

On July 7, 1903, Mother Jones led her "textile army," with about 50 children and 150 adults, on the first leg of

The march gave the kids a welcome break from their hard labor.

the march. The children carried knapsacks that each held a tin cup, a plate, and a fork and a knife, and they hoisted banners that read, WE WANT TIME TO PLAY and WE WANT TIME TO GO TO SCHOOL. Some children were dressed as Revolutionary War soldiers, and several boys played fifes and drums in the textile army's colorful band.

The children were eager to go—for many, it would be their first journey from home—but the march would be far from easy. When it was not blistering hot, it was pouring rain. Torrential downpours soaked the tents that the marchers slept in at night. Making things worse, mosquitoes attacked them after the rains stopped. The itching was unbearable. "From time to time we had to send some of the children back to their homes," Mother Jones recalled. "They were too weak to stand the march."

Another occasional problem was a lack of food. Mother Jones had hoped that farmers would feed the

President Theodore Roosevelt, left, and Vice President Charles Warren Fairbanks at the "Summer White House" in Oyster Bay, New York.

marchers as they passed by, but in these tough times, there were only a few who were able or willing to do so. After the supplies the marchers brought with them ran out, there was simply not enough food to satisfy all the grumbling stomachs. Mother Jones pleaded for food from grocers and union members, and the kids ate whatever was available; one time, they had ice cream and coffee for breakfast.

Still another problem was a lack of money. Everyday working people had little money to share with the marchers, and many who were wealthy refused to support their cause. Mother Jones did not even have enough money to pay the toll for the marchers to cross the Delaware Bridge. That problem was settled when a

The boys and girls would now march to President Theodore Roosevelt's summer house in Oyster Bay.

supporter stepped forward to help, but more than one hundred marchers dropped out of the protest by the end of the third day.

Things were looking bleak, morale was low, and success seemed impossible. Still the protesters who were strong enough to continue remained determined to draw the nation's attention to their cause. They marched on.

Things got better. Local labor unions and hotel managers started offering food, shelter, and money. Some of the donations came from people who had read about the march in the newspaper. This is what Mother Jones had counted on.

On good days, the children jumped into nearby rivers for a bath and a quick cooldown. Laughter and giggles filled the air as they splashed one another before heading back to the hot roads. On bad days, factory owners tried to prevent the young marchers from entering their towns. None of them succeeded.

On July 15, Mother Jones announced a dramatic change in plans—the boys and girls would now march to President Theodore Roosevelt's summer house in

Oyster Bay, New York. At the same time she publicized a letter that she had written to the president, seeking his help:

> We ask you, Mr. President, if our commercial greatness has not cost us too much by being built upon the quivering hearts of helpless children? We who know of these sufferings have taken up their cause and are now marching toward you in the hope that your tender heart will counsel with us to abolish this crime.

President Roosevelt did not reply to her letter, and his assistant said that the president would not meet with Mother Jones and the children.

Meanwhile, support for the marchers grew—but the weather took a turn for the worse. When the marchers arrived at Princeton, New Jersey, they were greeted with fierce winds and a driving rain. Weather conditions were so frightful that the caretaker of former President Grover Cleveland's home invited the marchers to sleep in the president's barn. The proprietor of the Nassau Inn on the Princeton square provided the marchers with their evening meal.

The following morning, Mother Jones spoke to a crowd that included professors from Princeton University. While delivering her speech, she pointed to James Ashworth, a ten-year-old marcher whose shoulders were stooped from carrying bundles of yarn that weighed seventy-five pounds. Mother Jones said that while the children of Princeton were studying in

But the day turned serious when Mother Jones gave a speech at the zoo.

comfortable schools, James was earning barely three dollars a week working ten hours a day in a carpet factory.

"That night," Mother Jones recalled, "we camped on the banks of Stony Brook, where years and years before, the ragged Revolutionary Army camped, Washington's brave soldiers that made their fight for freedom."

In New York City, the children were amazed at the sight of the massive skyscrapers. As they had done in other towns, they formed a parade to announce their arrival. The band led the way, and then came the children with picket signs. Local child workers also jumped into the procession.

On Twentieth Street, Mother Jones gave another speech, this time to about two thousand people. After her speech, the child marchers held an American flag at its corners to catch coins tossed by supporters. By the end of the collection, the flag looked like a big bag full of money.

Many people volunteered to open their homes and food pantries to the marchers. The children were happy with the growing support, and their smiles grew even bigger the following day when they visited Coney Island. This seaside amusement park offered carnival

Mother Jones usually marched in an antique black dress with a high lace collar.

rides and a wild animal show featuring lions, tigers, elephants, and monkeys. Some of the children said that they wished they could stay with the show rather than return to Philadelphia.

But the day turned serious when Mother Jones gave a speech at the zoo. She found some empty cages and instructed a few children to go inside them to show the crowds of people how in the textile factories, the children's lives were like those of caged animals. "We want President Roosevelt to hear the wail of the children who never have a chance to go to school," she said.

President Roosevelt said nothing about the marching children, and his personal secretary warned that the group would not be welcome in Oyster Bay. But Mother Jones and her textile army, which now numbered only two dozen or so, marched on.

On July 28, Mother Jones, three children, and a few adults quietly approached the president's summer home. The president's personal secretary did meet with them, but he quickly turned them away, saying the president was not available.

For three long weeks, the children had marched miles after miles and endured awful hardships. Now, it all seemed so worthless. The president had ignored them.

Hurt and humiliated, the children boarded a train for the trip home. Mother Jones did her best to comfort them. She told them that the march brought their difficult lives to the nation's attention. She said she would write another letter to the president. She declared they would organize a bigger, better march, this one in Washington, DC.

The proposed march never happened. Mother Jones moved on to other strikes in other parts of the country. Back in Philadelphia, the owners of the textile factories crushed the strikes. The children and their families went back to work under the same conditions and for the same number of hours.

The child marchers of 1903 did not succeed in the short term, but two years later, Pennsylvania raised the minimum work age from thirteen to fourteen. While it might sound like a small victory, the new law made it possible for thousands of younger children to go to school and play at recess—kids who otherwise would have been toiling in the mills, some of them the younger siblings of those who had marched. O

CHAPTER TWO

The Bonus March

1932
*Waters begins the journey
to Washington, DC*

1930   1935   1940

Nobody would have guessed it from looking at their scrawny bodies, but at the tender age of seven, Nick and Joe Oliver were veteran boxers. By 1932, the twin brothers had already been boxing for about two years.

Their father, Anthony, managed their careers in the family's hometown of Belle Vernon, Pennsylvania, about thirty-five miles southeast of Pittsburgh. But truth be told, their careers didn't require a whole lot of managing.

Anthony usually set up makeshift boxing rings throughout the Belle Vernon area, and small crowds of people would show up for the odd spectacle of two small brothers pummeling each other for three rounds. The boys really boxed, too; they didn't fake it. But they didn't hurt each other, either.

Spectators loved watching the twins and showered them with cheers and applause. After the final bell rang, Anthony always announced that both boys had won. The match was a draw. It was always a draw, even though each brother thought for sure that he was better than the other.

The Olivers didn't do all this just for fun. They did it for cash. At the end of each match, Anthony took up a collection from the crowd. It was an honest way for the Olivers to earn some extra money—Nick and Joe had six other siblings—during a time of harsh poverty.

Although the Oliver family, all ten of them, had a place to call home, they struggled to make ends meet on a daily basis.

In the 1930s, the United States was in the midst of the Great Depression. Many workers had lost their jobs, their incomes, and their ability to provide for themselves and their families.

Poverty-stricken workers also lost their homes. In 1932, far more than a million people, including two hundred thousand boys and girls, were homeless. Many of them ended up living in poorly built shacks in impoverished communities they called Hoovervilles. That was their way of blaming President Herbert Hoover for not doing enough to help them secure employment.

Military veterans were especially angry at the president. They were upset not only about the lack of jobs, but also about the government's refusal to pay them for having served in World War I.

Nine years earlier, Congress had agreed to pass a bill granting war veterans either $1.00 per day for domestic service (serving in the United States) or $1.25 per day for serving overseas. The bill also said that if a veteran's

The Oliver twins boxing to raise money at a Bonus Army camp.

calculated payment was less than fifty dollars, the government must pay him immediately, but those who earned more than that would not receive their money until 1945.

Many veterans needed the money *immediately*, in 1932, not in thirteen years. Nick and Joe's father was among those veterans. He had served in an army tank battalion during the war, and like other veterans, he was in urgent need of money. Although the Oliver family, all ten of them, had a place to call home, they struggled to make ends meet on a daily basis.

Across the country, in Portland, Oregon, former army sergeant Walter W. Waters had a bold idea. On March 15, 1932, while speaking at a meeting of disgruntled veterans, Waters asked the group to join him in traveling to the US Capitol and demanding immediate cash payment of the money.

The veterans weren't enthusiastic about the idea, but they changed their minds two months later, when the US House of Representatives chose not to pass a bill that would have allowed for immediate payment of the cash due them. Opponents of the bill called the money a "bonus," extra payment for what should have been freely given patriotic service.

On May 11, the day of the House's decision, Waters and about three hundred veterans headed to the local train yards to begin the journey to Washington, DC, almost three thousand miles away. Leading the way was a banner that read, PORTLAND BONUS MARCH—ON TO WASHINGTON. The veterans had thirty dollars among them, not enough even to buy food for the trip, let alone train tickets.

The following day, they hopped aboard freight cars made available by railroad workers who supported their cause. The cars smelled of fresh cow manure, but the members of the Bonus Expeditionary Force— the protesting veterans named themselves after the troops sent overseas in World War I—were happy for the ride.

The Bonus Army received additional support along the way. Newspapers publicized the trip, railroad

... thousands of other jobless veterans also decided to head to the nation's capital.

workers made space on their cars, and cheering supporters offered food. Some governors also provided trucks to move the Bonus Army through their states as quickly as possible.

Another remarkable thing happened: thousands of other jobless veterans also decided to head to the nation's capital. From all across the country, they hitchhiked, hopped on trains, and formed convoys of dilapidated cars and trucks.

Nick and Joe's father, Anthony Oliver, was a member of American Legion, a group of World War I veterans who gathered together socially and for the benefit of helping one another. His chapter, Post 669, supported the immediate payment of the bonus and asked Anthony and his friend Sam Ditz to travel to Washington, DC, and represent the post in the Bonus Army. Anthony and Ditz agreed to go.

The first group of Bonus marchers arrived in Washington, DC, on May 23. By the time the Portland

Neighborhood kids, upper left, watching a Bonus Army march.

crew got there six days later, there were several hundred veterans waiting to greet them with cheers, handshakes, and backslaps.

Evalyn Walsh McClean, who owned the world's most famous jewels, including the Hope Diamond, was at home on Massachusetts Avenue when Bonus Army trucks rumbled into the city. She was so moved at seeing the poor veterans that she went to a local diner and ordered one thousand sandwiches for them.

DC Chief of Police Pelham D. Glassford supplied them with hot coffee. Glassford had also served in World War I, and he wanted to support the veterans while also keeping order and maintaining safety. He even helped set up camps where the Bonus Army would live.

Before long, more than fifteen thousand veterans and their families, including young children—and the Olivers—had streamed into the nation's capital.

Nick, Joe, Anthony, and Ditz left for Washington at the end of the school year. One day in May, right around dawn, the twins followed their father out the door and climbed into his Model A Ford. Anthony started the engine with a crank, and off they all went.

Nick and Joe had no idea what the bonus was all about. Nor did they understand the Bonus Army. But they were really excited to be heading to the nation's capital; they'd never been there before.

The trip to Washington was 250 miles long. Along the way, the Oliver boys picnicked on potatoes, salami, and bread. Anthony knew that the food would not last long, and he occasionally pulled to the side of the road so that the twins could jump out and grab some apples and berries.

"I remember when we saw the Capitol," Joe recalled years later. "My eyes popped out."

The Olivers joined the veterans and their families as they got settled. With help from Chief Glassford, some of the veterans set up living quarters in abandoned buildings on government property. Others pitched tents in public parks. Most built makeshift shacks in an area called Anacostia Flats. Veterans and their families used whatever they could find to build their shacks— bedsprings, hubcaps, tin cans, fence stakes, car seats, even egg cartons.

The Oliver twins slept in their father's car for the first few nights. After that, they slept in a lean-to made of thick cardboard in the area of Anacostia they called Camp Marks. This campground was on the other side of the Anacostia River from downtown Washington. A wooden drawbridge connected the two areas.

About 15,000 people—including 1,100 women and children—lived in the camp, and they made it as comfortable as possible. At its peak, the camp had its own dining facilities, a post office, a library, a barbershop, a doctor's office, and a school. Unlike the US Army and Washington, DC, Camp Marks was not racially segregated. People of all ethnicities lived, worked, and played together.

During the day, many of the men left camp to find work that usually paid them about two dollars per day. That is what Anthony did, and while he was at work, Nick and Joe roamed around the camp, played along the river, or helped out with small jobs here and there.

The Oliver twins also regularly boxed for the Bonus marchers. Anthony made a ring, the boys went three rounds, and the Bonus veterans tossed coins into a passing hat. According to Nick, the boys once "got one dollar and thirty-seven cents in dimes, nickels, and pennies," equivalent to more than twenty-four dollars in 2020.

On June 7, more than five thousand veterans and their families assembled at the Washington Monument for their first major protest. Beginning at 7:00 p.m., they marched down Pennsylvania Avenue toward the Capitol.

At the head of the march were banners calling for immediate payment of the bonus. Then came a large group of veterans who had won medals for bravery in

Bonus Army families took shelter in tents, sheds, and shacks.

World War I. Following these war heroes were six regiments and their families, all marching in line. A group of trucks carried men with disabilities, highlighting those who had been wounded in service to their country. Their injuries made it even harder, if not impossible, for them to land the jobs they so desperately needed.

The former soldiers were clean-shaven and well kempt, but their poverty was unmistakable. Some wore tattered uniforms from their days in the army, and

25

While many people sympathized with the marchers, the Bonus Army also had its detractors.

others had shirts that were frayed and badly wrinkled. Their hats and shoes were plagued with holes, and elbow patches were aplenty. The women and children also looked down-and-out.

Although the march included a small drum corps, the veterans walked in silence to demonstrate the seriousness of their needs. To some of the one hundred thousand spectators, the former soldiers and their families seemed sad and hopeless. No one cheered.

While many people sympathized with the marchers, the Bonus Army also had its detractors. Some believed that the government should never give cash to poor people; they decried the veterans as a bunch of un-American bums looking for a handout. Others feared that communists—who called for governments to seize private property and distribute it to citizens according to their need—were the real leaders of the Bonus Army. The Military Intelligence Division of the US Army even reported that communists were planning a revolution against the US government. Political leaders took this report seriously because communists had helped to lead a successful revolution in Russia in 1917, and Americans worried that if a similar revolution took

The Anacostia River was a favorite place for bathing, washing clothes, and swimming.

place in the United States, it would destroy the country they knew and loved. But Walter W. Waters, the head of the Bonus Army, was not a communist; he even kicked known communists out of the camp.

The US House of Representatives was about to vote on a bill authorizing immediate payment of the bonus, and before and after the June 7 march, veterans went to the US Capitol to speak with members of Congress about the vote. They lobbied congressmen and held sit-ins inside and outside the Capitol.

Moved by the veterans' arguments and plights, the House passed the bill on June 15. The Bonus Army had won its first battle.

Young boys, lower left, with the Bonus Army for a nighttime rally at the Capitol.

But the fight was far from over. Two days later, the Senate would vote on a similar bill. Unlike the House, where Democrats were the majority, the Senate held many Republicans who believed that immediate payment of the bonus would be too expensive for the government. Beyond the Senate, President Hoover also opposed the bill because he believed that it was not the government's responsibility to give cash to poor people.

As the Senate prepared to vote on June 17, thousands of veterans and their families poured onto the steps of the Capitol and into nearby areas. The crowds became so large that the police pulled up the drawbridge leading to Camp Marks, preventing about ten thousand more protesters from joining.

The Senate voted on the bill around 8:00 p.m., and Waters entered the Capitol to learn the result. Outside, he stepped onto a pedestal to deliver the news. The massive crowd grew quiet.

"Prepare yourselves for a disappointment, men," he said. "The Bonus has been defeated, 62 to 18."

The veterans were stunned at the lopsided vote. They couldn't believe that their senators had failed them so badly. Several protesters began to shout, and it seemed as if violence was about to erupt.

Waters understood the fury, but he warned against rioting and asked the veterans to prove the nation's faith in them by marching peacefully back to camp. Someone blew a bugle, and the veterans took off their caps, placed their hands over their hearts, and sang "America the Beautiful."

Oh, beautiful for heroes proved

In liberating strife,

Who more than self their country loved,

And mercy more than life!

America! America!

May God thy gold refine,

Till all success be nobleness,

And ev'ry gain divine.

Though defeated and disappointed, the veterans and their families persevered, doing what they could to keep the nation's attention on their cause. They published their own newspaper and broadened their pleas, calling for the government to help "all suffering Americans." They also staged individual protests. One veteran attracted publicity by burying himself in the ground with just a pipe sticking out so he could access air, food, and water.

The Oliver twins kept boxing.

The Bonus Army celebrated small victories, like the birth of the first "Bonus Baby" at the end of June, but poor living conditions became overwhelming. The oppressive heat and humidity of July wore them out. Their tents and shacks leaked in rainstorms and shook with the wind. Because there was little plumbing, conditions grew more and more unsanitary. Boys and girls suffered from head lice. Food grew scarce, and donations declined.

Chief of Police Glassford encouraged the veterans to leave the city, and in early July, Congress authorized

As tensions grew, arrests became common.

money to help transport them back home. Nick and Joe's father refused to back down. When just a few hundred veterans accepted the offer, political leaders began to ban them from public grounds.

These actions only served to increase the Bonus Army's determination. In mid-July, after being told they had to leave the area, veterans from California stood in a circle around the Capitol for three days. Thousands of others also continued to protest at the Capitol, even as police officers tried to drive them away.

As tensions grew, arrests became common. Glassford arrested Waters twice after he refused orders to leave Capitol grounds. Bonus marchers were also jailed when they tried to protest at the White House.

President Hoover detested the Bonus Army, and in late July, he ordered the DC police to expel veterans who occupied downtown buildings. Glassford managed to give the veterans several extra days to leave. But the delay didn't change anything. The veterans voted to stay put.

On the morning of July 28, Glassford and one hundred police officers removed veterans from the old armory, the largest of the buildings they occupied. Thousands of protesters assembled nearby, and someone began throwing bricks at the officers. In response, the police used nightsticks to beat back the protesters.

Veterans began to fight with one another in a building near the armory. When police went inside to investigate, gunfire erupted. It's not clear who shot first, but the incident left one veteran dead and three officers injured.

Meanwhile, US Army troops from Fort Myer, Virginia, were gathering in a grassy area between the White House and the Washington Monument. President Hoover had directed General Douglas MacArthur—who would later become a World War II hero—to use the troops to drive all veterans out of downtown Washington.

In the late afternoon, two hundred cavalry troops, three hundred infantrymen, and five tanks headed toward the busy streets. With their sabers drawn, the cavalry charged toward the crowds. Screams erupted as the veterans and their wives and children rushed to avoid the crush of the horses. The children ran as fast as their little legs would allow them.

Then the infantry, now wearing gas masks, threw tear-gas grenades inside buildings occupied by the veterans. They set fire to tents and shanties, while tanks armed with machine guns stood ready to shoot at any resisters.

One woman pleaded with a solider to allow her to retrieve clothes for herself and her child from her shack. The soldier refused and torched the shack and all her belongings.

Black smoke filled the skies, and veterans, families, and spectators coughed and collapsed as tear gas filled their lungs.

Several hours later, the troops had satisfied President Hoover's demand—they had cleared the downtown area of two thousand veterans and their families. But General MacArthur, acting against the president's orders, pressed on toward the shanties and tents at Camp Marks in Anacostia. He wanted the veterans to leave not only downtown but every place they occupied.

Before heading across the bridge, the troops paused to rest. They also wanted to give the residents of Camp Marks time to pack their belongings and leave before the torching began. Some troop members had mixed feelings about the mission. They knew they were supposed to follow orders, but they regretted treating the veterans so poorly.

Nick and Joe Oliver were asleep at the time. Back home, they usually went to bed later than they did at the camp, but Camp Marks was really dark at night, and they didn't have a flashlight or a lantern. "All you could do was hit the sack," Nick said years later.

Their father woke them up as the troops approached. "Come on!" he shouted. "Come on! The soldiers are going to kill us. Let's get out of here."

The boys jumped up, gathered a few things, and hopped into the car. Lucky for them, it was right next to the lean-to. Anthony cranked the engine and tore out of the camp.

They could see other families scurrying here and there. They looked panicked and scared.

At 9:00 p.m., the soldiers crossed into Anacostia and fired tear-gas grenades toward veterans who had

Most of the American public eventually sided with the Bonus Army.

refused to leave. They set fire to every camp they could find. The Olivers' lean-to went up in flames.

Fleeing veterans and their families headed toward the Maryland border, where the National Guard waited to transport them to Pennsylvania. From there, they could make arrangements to go home.

The March of the Bonus Army had come to an inglorious end.

General MacArthur met with the press around 11:00 p.m. "Had the President not acted today, had he permitted this thing to go on for twenty-four hours more, he would have been faced with a grave situation which would have caused a real battle," MacArthur said. "Had he let it go on another week, I believe the institutions of our Government would have been severely threatened."

There was no evidence to back MacArthur's argument. Nor was there evidence to support the claim that revolutionaries were in charge of the Bonus Army. Most of the American public eventually sided with the Bonus

Army. When movie theaters showed film clips of the July 28 expulsion, audiences booed MacArthur and the US Army. Several months later, voters removed President Hoover from office and elected his Democratic opponent, Franklin D. Roosevelt. Political reporters suggested that Hoover's hostility toward the Bonus Army had ensured his defeat.

Like Hoover, President Roosevelt opposed immediate payment of the bonus. But unlike his predecessor, the newly elected president quickly created job programs for the unemployed.

Three years later, despite the president's disapproval, Congress passed legislation granting immediate cash payment of the bonus. Finally, in June 1936, members of the Bonus Army, and all World War I veterans, began to cash their checks.

Anthony Oliver was among the happy recipients. Nick and Joe were amazed when their father showed them a fan of hundred-dollar bills. It was a lot more than they had ever made in the boxing ring. ○

CHAPTER THREE

The Strike for a Better School

1951

*The student planning
committee leads the way*

○

1950   1955   1960

"I'm sick and tired of it all."

It was early in the 1950–1951 school year, and fifteen-year-old Barbara Johns was already disgusted with her school. A serious student, she wasn't upset with her teachers, her classmates, or even the demands of studying. Johns was sick and tired of the facilities and resources at her all-Black high school: Robert Russa Moton High School in Farmville, Virginia.

Everything about the single-story building was far too small. It had been built in 1939 to hold 200 students, but the school's population was now about 450, making the students feel like gumballs in a candy machine. Some teachers held their classes in the auditorium. Others used an abandoned school bus.

A few years earlier, the school board had responded to the need for extra classrooms only by building three tar-paper shacks next to the main building, which did little to solve the school's space crisis. Worse, the shacks made the students feel as if they weren't worthy of anything more than a pen built for animals. The students referred to them as "chicken coops."

They had roofs that leaked in rainstorms. If students weren't moving water pails to catch the drips, they were holding umbrellas over their desks so that the ink on their papers wouldn't smudge.

Barbara Johns graduated in 1952 from Alabama State Laboratory High School.

Black smoke created an ash that covered everything and filled the lungs of students and teachers.

The shacks were poorly heated by wood-burning potbellied stoves in the center of each one. Students who sat right next to the stoves suffered from unbearable heat, while those farther away shivered. Black smoke created an ash that covered everything and filled the lungs of students and teachers. All the wheezing and coughing in the packed classrooms made for a terribly unhealthy situation.

"Then there were the smells," recalls former student John Stokes. "Mix the peculiar odor of tar paper with the exhaust from the school buses and fumes from the potbellied stove, and you have a pretty obnoxious odor that students had to endure day in and day out." Moton had neither a school nurse nor even a room where students could lie down and recover.

The main school building lacked other basic facilities. There was no cafeteria for making hot food. Students who did not bring their lunches could purchase only the items on the menu: milk and a bun. Bathrooms were also few and far between, and of the four water fountains for the 450 students, two were broken.

In addition, the building did not have a gymnasium or locker rooms. Student athletes sometimes changed into and out of their uniforms on school buses. There was no industrial-arts shop where students could learn trades. Students interested in the sciences had no access to proper labs, and there was only one microscope in the entire school. Former student Edwilda Allen recalls that "the only person who had the microscope was the teacher and she had the frog and we all had to gather around to see her dissect it."

Moton did not have enough books for its students, either. Most of the books that were available had been handed down by white schools. Tattered and torn, these books had vulgar drawings and racial slurs on the margins of their pages.

All these things, in and of themselves, infuriated Barbara Johns. But there was something else that troubled her: Farmville High School, the school for white kids, had everything that Moton did not.

The US Supreme Court had declared years earlier that it was legally acceptable for public schools to be racially segregated as long as they were equal. But it was clear to Johns that Moton's facilities and resources were unequal to those enjoyed by the white students at Farmville High.

Miss Inez Davenport, Johns's favorite teacher, was also well aware of Moton's inferior resources. She was a music teacher without proper teaching tools. She had been able to build a school choir—student voices did not cost money—but she didn't have instruments to form a band, because the school board had deemed them an unnecessary luxury for Black students.

One day, after hearing Johns and her friends complain about Moton, Miss Davenport offered a simple suggestion. "Why don't you do something about it?" she said.

The question stung Johns, and she turned and walked away, thinking that her trusted teacher was dismissing her concerns.

But that wasn't the case at all. Miss Davenport wasn't being sarcastic, she was truly suggesting that Johns and her friends come up with their own plan. She wanted her students to think for themselves, to stand up on their own, and to take control of their lives.

Johns thought long and hard about the question, and in conversation with Miss Davenport, she grew to see it as a sincere invitation to action. Her teacher had not failed her after all; she had empowered her.

Johns and her family lived about fifteen miles from Moton, in a small farmhouse in a rural area called Darlington Heights. Her father, Robert Melvin Johns, was a farmer, and her mother, Violet Adele Johns, was a clerk with the US Navy Department in Washington, DC. Her mother lived in Washington, nearly two hundred miles away, during the week, so Barbara was responsible for many of the household chores—chopping wood, gardening, cooking, and cleaning.

Students in a classroom in the main building of the Robert R. Moton High School.

When her father was working in the fields, as he was most of the day, Johns was also responsible for caring for her younger siblings: her sister Joan, a first-year student at Moton, and her brothers Ernest and Roderick, both elementary school students. On school mornings, Johns woke up early so that she would have plenty of time to get everyone ready. While she was conscientious in fulfilling her duties, she sometimes neglected to take care of herself as well as she cared for others.

That's what happened one October morning in 1950. After packing lunch for everyone, Johns and her siblings headed toward the bus stop just down the hill from their house. Then she realized that she had forgotten her own lunch. She trekked home but didn't make it back in time. She had missed the bus.

This posed a major problem. The bus for Black students was dilapidated and crowded, but it was the one and only bus for Black students in her neighborhood. Stranded, Johns decided to stay put and see if a car might come by and offer her a ride.

While she was waiting, the "whites only" school bus that carried white students to Farmville High drove right by her without stopping. Johns noticed that unlike her bus, the one for white students was in excellent condition, and it was also only half full.

As the bus passed her by, Johns grew angry—and determined. "Right then and there," she recalled, "I decided something had to be done about this inequality—but I still didn't know what."

By the next morning, Johns did know. "As I lay in bed that night, I prayed for help. That night, whether in a dream or whether I was awake—but I felt I was awake—a plan began to formulate in my mind, a plan I felt was divinely inspired, because I hadn't been able to think of anything until then." The plan was to call together a group of student leaders and ask them to help her carry out a student strike for a new high school.

But something human might also have been at work. Miss Davenport later said that months earlier she had told Johns and others about a group of students in Massachusetts who had gone on strike to win higher salaries for their teachers. "If they can do that, so can you," Davenport remembered saying.

Johns contacted three important student leaders: seniors John Watson, Carrie Stokes, and John Stokes.

Together, the four held a meeting at the athletic field and agreed on the need for a strike.

"It was about a quality education," recalled Watson. "We could no longer get the quality education we needed in this building."

"We wanted so much here and had so little," Johns explained years later. "We had talents and abilities here that weren't being realized."

The four students decided to hold the strike in late spring. They believed that the need to make sure seniors graduated on time would make the school board more willing to meet their demands.

The four then shared the news with the other student leaders they had selected to become part of the planning committee, including representatives from each grade. When the time was right, these responsible boys and girls would inform the rest of their class about the strike.

Edwilda Allen, the eighth-grade representative, was struck by the boldness of Johns's plan. "We were taught to be obedient and respectful, and there she was, asking us to be disobedient," Allen said. "It was shocking."

Johns's plan took on new urgency on March 13, 1951, when one of the run-down school buses stalled on the train tracks. A train slammed into the bus, killing five children, three from the same family: Naomi Hendricks, Christine Hendricks, Dodson Hendricks, Whitfield Page, and Hettie Dungee. They were Johns's friends. Heartbroken, she was more determined than ever to stage a strike for an equal school, one that was as good as the white school.

Strike organizer John Watson and friends in front of a tarpaper shack at Moton High School.

Planning intensified in the following weeks. From the beginning, the students had vowed to keep the plan secret. They spoke about it in codes. According to John Stokes, "We called our secret plan the 'Manhattan Project,' adopting the code name given to the top-secret effort developed by the United States and some of its allies during World War II to produce the first nuclear weapons." The students insisted on secrecy because they worried that if adults knew about their plans, they would try to stop them.

But there was one adult with whom Johns shared the secret—Miss Davenport. Throughout the planning

Fear was in the air as students worried whether they would be jailed for their actions.

stages, Johns asked her for advice about the strike. At first, the two talked together quietly in Miss Davenport's classroom. But later, fearing they would be caught, they exchanged secret notes in a music book they passed back and forth.

On the day before the strike, the planning committee met at John and Carrie Stokes's family farm. Fear was in the air as students worried whether they would be jailed for their actions. Jails were dangerous places for Black people. White guards often brutalized Black prisoners, and there was no one to stop this from happening. Their fears were calmed, at least a bit, when the Stokes siblings' older brother Leslie said that the Farmville jail was far too small to fit all 450 Moton students. After checking the weather and reviewing everyone's responsibilities, the students disbanded, eager for the morning but uncertain about how the day would unfold.

DAY ONE

April 23 finally arrived. The day started off normally. The halls were crowded, students were laughing, and teachers were sipping coffee.

Students disembarking their bus near one of the school's tarpaper shacks.

Amid the morning routines, John Watson and two other students sneaked off campus to carry out the important task of tricking Principal Jones into leaving the school.

"We had to get him off campus, because we knew if Mr. Jones was on campus, there was no way there was going to be a strike," Watson explained. "He was a very strong leader, and a very highly respected man."

Watson's job was to call Principal Jones and pretend to be a businessman who had spotted Moton students skipping school. As Watson now headed toward a pay phone, the other two students positioned themselves on the only routes that the principal would take if he were to leave campus. Their mission was to report any sighting of Principal Jones.

Tucked into a public phone booth, Watson nervously dialed the numbers to Principal Jones's office. He had originally hesitated to accept the job, worried the principal would recognize his voice. But Johns suggested he hold a handkerchief over the phone to muffle it. With the handkerchief in place, he told Principal Jones that there was a disturbance at the Greyhound bus terminal involving a few Moton students. "Would you please come down and take care of it?" Watson asked.

Davenport—whose office was right next to the principal's—heard Jones slam his door on the way out, and Johns soon received confirmation from Watson and his friends that the principal had indeed left the campus.

Johns then instructed several students to deliver notes to each classroom. The notes, which she had written, stated that teachers should immediately send their students to the auditorium for an 11:00 assembly. The teachers had no reason to doubt the messages. Assemblies were typically held at that time. Plus, Johns had signed each of the notes with a *J*, just as Principal Jones usually signed his notes.

Teachers and students soon began filing into the auditorium. As John Stokes remembers the scene, "We were packed in that room like sardines in a can."

When everyone was finally seated, the stage curtain opened, and much to the surprise of the students and teachers in the auditorium, Principal Jones was nowhere in sight. The students who had planned the strike sat in a row of folding chairs at center stage.

John Stokes stood up, quieted everyone, and asked them to stand and recite the Pledge of Allegiance and the Lord's Prayer. He then led them in an opening song.

As the students sat back down, Johns moved to the podium. Her sister, Joan, could not believe it. "What is going on?" she thought. "Why is she up there?"

Johns spoke forcefully. First, she asked the teachers to leave the auditorium. "This is for the students," she said. "This isn't for you." All but one of the teachers complied, and the one who remained was soon escorted out by a few football players.

With the teachers gone, Johns told the students that the time had come for them to do something about the horrible conditions of their school. She went through a long list of the school's problems, then compared Moton to Farmville High, and finally reminded her peers that Moton students had a constitutional right to equal facilities.

The students were shocked. Was this the same Barbara Johns who had seemed so quiet, so reserved, before this assembly?

Johns continued with confidence. The adults, she said, had tried to convince the school board to build a new high school for them, and because they had failed, it was now the students' responsibility to take matters into their own hands. "We have to make a change, and I mean now!"

Johns explained that she wanted the entire student body to go on strike until the school board agreed to build a new high school for Black students.

And then Principal Jones returned. He realized he'd been tricked, and he was not happy. He told the students that he and other adults had been working on the problems, and that they should go back to class and be patient.

Johns did not back down, and she calmly but forcefully asked Principal Jones to return to his office. It took him a while, but he finally realized that Johns was in control of the room, and that the students were definitely not going back to their classrooms. With the situation out of his hands, Principal Jones left the auditorium.

The student body rumbled, and Johns took her shoe and pounded it on the podium to bring the meeting back to order.

Her sister was afraid. "What's going to happen to us now?" Joan wondered. Other students felt the same, and at least one asked Johns about the dangers of going on strike.

"What if they put us in jail?" the student asked.

Johns's answer was the one she'd heard the day before—the Farmville jail was too small to hold 450 Moton students.

Students started to shout out their excitement about the strike. Carl Allen, an enthusiastic supporter of Johns's plan, remembers students saying, "Strike the school!" John Stokes recalls that the assembly turned into a pep rally, with students chanting, "Two bits, four bits, six bits, a dollar! All for this strike, stand up and holler!"

"Don't be afraid," Johns told the boisterous crowd. "Just follow us out." The student planning committee led the way, and the entire student body followed.

Outside, students grabbed picket signs the committee had made: DOWN WITH TARPAPER SHACKS and WE WANT A NEW SCHOOL OR NONE AT ALL. With their signs raised high, students marched around the school.

At last, Johns's secret had turned into a full-blown

At last, Johns's secret had turned into a full-blown protest.

protest. Johns led her own march to the downtown office of the school superintendent, T. J. McIlwaine. But when they arrived, McIlwaine refused to meet them. This was the first major obstruction that the students encountered, and it came as a surprise to Johns. During the planning, she thought, "People would hear us, would see us and understand our difficulty, would sympathize with our plight and would grant us our new school building. It would be grand, and we would live happily ever after."

Disappointed but not defeated, Johns's group marched back to campus, where students were still picketing. The strike leaders then held a meeting in the library to discuss their next steps. One of the leaders suggested the committee stop everything until parents gave their permission to proceed. The comment brought the meeting to a standstill, and the committee decided it needed outside help and guidance.

A committee member telephoned the Reverend L. Francis Griffin, the Black minister at First Baptist Church in Farmville, and asked him to meet with the students. They had turned to Griffin partly because he was a Parent Teacher Association (PTA) leader who had already petitioned the school board for a new building.

Griffin accepted the invitation, and arrived at the library within the hour. Seeing that the students were still ground to a halt, he advised the group to take a vote and accept the decision of the majority. The students did, and decided to proceed without receiving permission from their parents.

Griffin offered one more piece of advice: Call the state office of the National Association for the Advancement of Colored People (NAACP). Griffin was founder and president of the Farmville chapter of the NAACP, and he was sure that the organization's civil rights lawyers in Richmond could help.

NAACP attorney Oliver Hill was in the Richmond office when Johns called. "She wanted us to take her case and handle it," Hill recalled in 2004. "She was so insistent."

Hill did not commit to taking the case, and after the call, Johns grabbed a pen and, with help from Carrie Stokes, drafted a letter to the NAACP lawyers. "Due to the fact that the facilities and building in the name of Robert R. Moton High School are inadequate, we understand that your help is available to us," she wrote. "Please we beg you to come down at the first of this week." Johns even offered the attorneys a place to stay overnight.

"Carrie typed it up," John Stokes later said, "and then one of the committee members took it directly to the post office. We felt we couldn't trust any outsider, not even the postman."

The student leaders rejoined hundreds of their classmates outside until the school day ended. That evening, Johns, like most other students, had a lot of explaining to do. Her father listened intently as she explained the strike and her leading role. She spoke with passion,

Moton High School students, including those who took part in the historic strike.

intensity, and stubborn determination. He could easily see that there was no way to dissuade his daughter. Johns would fight on.

DAY TWO

John Stokes was concerned that the strike would not hold and students would go back to school. So starting on the second day, he and his friends kept their eyes on the buses—which despite the strike kept their normal schedules—to see if any students were returning to Moton. If they spotted any, Stokes and his friends would stop the bus, escort the students off, and then drive them back home, using cars and trucks provided by supportive adults.

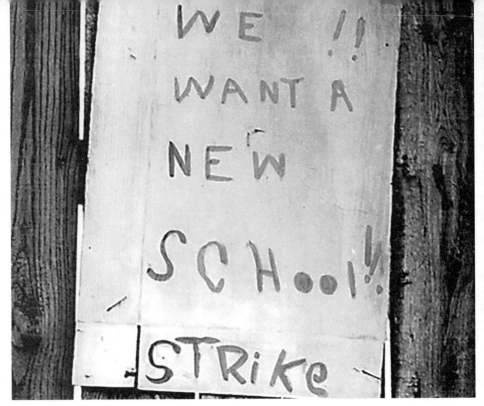

A handmade protest sign announcing the strike.

The strike committee met at Griffin's church for another strategy session. In the afternoon, about twenty of them marched downtown to insist on a meeting with Superintendent McIlwaine. This time, he agreed to meet them at the nearby courthouse.

The students were nervous. They had never confronted a white leader, let alone the head of the school system. Making matters worse, Superintendent McIlwaine was already irritated.

But Johns did not let his impatient, unfriendly attitude frighten her. With her typical poise, she explained why Moton was not acceptable, and then she delivered the final punch.

We demand a new school, she concluded.

The superintendent was far from sympathetic. He told Johns that the school board already had plans for a new school for the Moton students, and that the students would have to be patient and wait for the board to finalize everything.

"You upstarts!" he said. "You need to go back to school before all your parents are in jail."

The students came to attention. That was a scary threat, and they left the courthouse worried about their mothers and fathers, and unsure about what to do next.

DAY THREE

Good news arrived on Wednesday when Griffin told the strike committee that two NAACP attorneys, Oliver Hill and Spottswood Robinson, had agreed to meet with them that afternoon. The students cheered.

But the celebration did not last long. In the meeting, Hill and Robinson told the students that the NAACP would not help them fight for a new Moton that would be equal to Farmville High. They explained that the NAACP was focusing their efforts in court only on Black students who demanded an end to their racially segregated schools. The NAACP's goal was to prove that separate but equal could not exist, and that racial segregation in public schools was unconstitutional. Hill and Robinson then said that if they agreed to change their demand to a new racially integrated school, one attended by Black students and white students together, the NAACP might be able to help.

Johns was shocked. "Initially, nobody dared dream beyond a separate facility with proper equipment and good buildings," she recalled in 1988. "But once the lawyers explained that integration would be the best way for us to accomplish our goals, I said, 'Let's go for it all.'"

Not everyone felt the same way. Some of the student leaders were discouraged and unsure about changing their original demand for a new Moton High. After all, they loved their teachers and the spirit of their all-Black school. Why demand something that might take away the good with the bad?

The students debated for several hours before voting. Integration won by only one vote. The students were now demanding a new public school for all eligible students, no matter their race.

That was exciting enough. But shortly after the vote the students learned that another member of the NAACP would visit them the following day. Lester Banks, the executive secretary for the Virginia NAACP, had agreed to speak at a PTA meeting.

DAY FOUR AND BEYOND

About one thousand people turned out for the PTA meeting at First Baptist Church on Main Street to talk about the protest, and many of those in attendance were wearing their finest suits and dresses. Dressing up for community meetings was an honored practice at this point. Plus, serious business called for serious clothing.

Integration won by only one vote.

Johns held the audience's attention as she explained that after discussion with NAACP leaders, the students had changed their goal and were now seeking a new racially integrated school. She asked everyone to support the decision.

Lester Banks spoke next, and he threw his weight behind Johns and the students. "The problem is that a new colored high school will not bring you equality," he said. "When colored people are separated, we're stamped with a brand of inferiority."

Audience members expressed some concerns afterward, but they voted overwhelmingly to back what both the students and the NAACP were now asking for—permission to proceed with a lawsuit challenging racially segregated schools in their county.

Another mass meeting was held the following week, and this time even more people attended. NAACP attorneys Hill and Robinson were present, and they made the case, once again, for a lawsuit challenging segregated schools. Former Moton High principal Joseph Pervall accused the NAACP attorneys of unfairly changing the students' earlier demand for an all-Black school.

Johns would have none of it. She rose from her seat, strode to the podium, and said, "Don't let any Tom, Dick, or Harry Pervall stop you from supporting us!" The crowd roared its approval, and people lined up to sign the official petition demanding that the school board desegregate public schools throughout the county. "We had tears in our eyes as our parents signed," said John Stokes.

A few days later, Stokes received a disturbing call from his aunt. She told him that a cross was burning at Moton High. He slammed the phone down and rushed to the school. He knew that the Ku Klux Klan—the country's most prominent hate group—often burned crosses on the property of Black people as a way to terrorize them.

At the school, Stokes saw a charred cross that stood more than ten feet high. The fire had been extinguished, but gas-soaked rags still hung on its arms. The burned cross was a symbol of hatred directed at him and all Black people fighting for an integrated education.

But it did not stop the students and the NAACP.

On May 7, 1951, the NAACP filed an official petition with the school board. The legal case was now officially begun. With the case in process, the Moton students went back to school. Their remarkable strike had come to an end.

Sixteen days later, after board members had rejected the petition, the NAACP filed a federal lawsuit against the Prince Edward County school board. The lawsuit argued that the racially segregated schools in the county were unconstitutional.

Racist white people in the area were angry when they learned about the lawsuit, and they retaliated against the Black community who supported the students and the NAACP. The school board fired Principal Jones and other Black teachers. Bankers denied loans to Black families, and grocers stopped offering them credit. Johns's father, like many other Black workers, was not able to borrow the money he needed to buy food and other basic goods.

Johns suffered, too. Someone threatened her life, and her family grew so concerned for her safety that they sent her to live with her father's uncle, the Reverend Vernon Johns, and his family in Montgomery, Alabama. Vernon Johns was a civil rights activist who at the time was minister of the church where Martin Luther King Jr. would begin serving four years later.

Barbara Johns stayed in Montgomery. After graduating from high school there, she attended Spelman College, then a college for Black women, in Atlanta.

Meanwhile, the NAACP had taken the Moton case and combined it with four others into one lawsuit called *Brown v. Board of Education of Topeka, Kansas.* Like the Moton lawsuit, *Brown* argued that segregation in public schools was unconstitutional.

Back in Farmville, the school board acted as if they would win the pending lawsuit. They even built a new

Strike organizer John Stokes, second from left, and three other students surveying the cross burned at Moton High School.

high school for Black students to prove that it could provide a separate but equal education.

The new Moton High School opened in 1953. Although it had a cafeteria and a gymnasium, the school's books and science equipment were far inferior to those at Farmville High. Despite their new building, Moton students still received an unequal education.

On May 17, 1954, the US Supreme Court ruled in favor of the Moton students and all other Black students named in *Brown*. "In the field of public education, the doctrine of 'separate but equal' has no place," wrote Chief Justice Earl Warren. "Separate educational facilities are inherently unequal."

The strike begun by Johns three years earlier had succeeded in court.

Johns was at Spelman when the Court issued its opinion, and she and Joan celebrated over a phone call. But this celebration did not last, either. Not long after the Supreme Court's decision, Johns's family home burned to the ground. Black people in the area suspected that someone opposed to desegregation had intentionally set the fire.

Virginia resisted the Court decision by closing all public schools for five years. Black students who relied on public schools lost five entire years of education. It was an awful time for Black kids in Virginia.

After five years of hard resistance, Virginia finally surrendered to the Court's decision and began to establish integrated public schools. Today, thanks to Barbara Johns and the student strike of 1951, it is illegal for schools across Virginia, and throughout the United States, to discriminate against students because of the color of their skin.

Postscript: On February 23, 2017, Virginia Governor Terry McAuliffe officially renamed a government office building where state politicians had strategized about how to resist the *Brown* decision. The building, which houses the state's top attorney, is now named the Barbara Johns Building.

Barbara Johns died in 1991, but her sister attended the dedication ceremony. "In seeing an injustice, she decided to do something about it," Joan said. "She stood up for what she believed, and she made a difference." O

CHAPTER FOUR

The Children's Crusade

1963

Protest organizers arrive at campuses with signs saying, IT'S TIME!

1960   1965   1970

"**M**y mother had told me not to march and said I'd better not go to jail. But this just felt like something we were supposed to do." Shirley Holmes Sims was a student at Parker High School when she defied her mother's orders and participated in what would become the turning point of the Black civil rights movement—the 1963 Children's Crusade in Birmingham, Alabama.

Birmingham was not a welcoming place for Black Americans in 1963. Although this was nine years after the *Brown* decision, the state government of Alabama was resisting the court order demanding desegregation of their public schools. In addition, Birmingham's restaurants refused to serve Black people at lunch counters. Public swimming pools did not allow Black children to swim with white boys and girls. And many Black citizens also feared violence.

Birmingham's main civil rights leader, the Reverend Fred Shuttlesworth, invited Dr. Martin Luther King Jr. and his civil rights group, the Southern Christian Leadership Conference (SCLC), to help lead a campaign for equality. King accepted, and on April 3, 1963, he and Shuttlesworth began a series of protests that included sit-ins, marches, rallies, and a boycott of city businesses.

The campaign had a strong start, but on April 10, Public Safety Commissioner Eugene "Bull" Connor

When King was released from jail on April 20, his campaign was stalled.

secured a court order (an injunction) that prohibited the protests. Dr. King disobeyed the injunction, explaining, "We cannot in all good conscience obey such an injunction which is an unjust, undemocratic and unconstitutional misuse of the legal process."

After attempting to march again, fifty protesters, including King and his best friend, the Reverend Ralph Abernathy, were arrested. On the sixth day of his imprisonment, King released a letter that has become one of the most important documents in US history: "Letter from Birmingham Jail."

In the letter, he explained his reason for disobeying the court order. He distinguished just laws, which respect all people and apply to everyone, from unjust laws, which discriminate against minorities. King also said that everyone has a moral obligation to obey just laws (civil obedience) and to disobey unjust laws (civil disobedience).

When King was released from jail on April 20, his campaign was stalled. The number of protesters willing to be arrested was small, morale was low, and media attention had tapered off.

SCLC staffer James Bevel and Ike Reynolds of the Congress of Racial Equality (CORE) suggested enlisting Birmingham's Black children and youth. Bevel argued that young people had already participated in protests and that they were full of energy and enthusiasm. Plus, unlike their parents and other adults, young people did not have to worry about losing their jobs as a result of protesting. They could protest, and even face arrest, without creating financial hardship on themselves or their families.

At first King was hesitant, but he eventually gave Bevel and Reynolds permission to organize a rally for young people during school hours on May 2. The two activists, along with Dorothy Cotton, Andrew Young, and others, immediately began to get the message out. Local deejays interspersed rock records with statements about freedom and announcements about the coming demonstration. They built excitement by calling the first day of the protest "D-Day" and "the party in the park." As a result, thousands of students, including children in elementary schools, attended the mass meetings and participated in training sessions in nonviolence.

Some of these young people faced resistance from their families. King later recalled the case of a teenage boy whose father had forbidden him to participate in the protests.

"'Daddy,' the boy said, 'I don't want to disobey you, but I have made my pledge. If you try to keep me home, I will sneak off. If you think I deserve to be punished for that, I'll just have to take the punishment. For, you see, I'm not doing this only because I want to be free. I'm doing this also because I want freedom for you and Mama, and I want it to come before you die'" The father changed his mind and approved of his son's decision.

Not every parent could be persuaded. Nor could some newspaper reporters. When they claimed King was unnecessarily exposing children to danger, he replied: "Where had these writers been . . . during the centuries when our segregated social system had been misusing and abusing Negro children?"

Other critics charged King with using the children as tools to make himself important. "The children understood the stakes they were fighting for," King later said. They all knew they were fighting for freedom.

Years later, Gwen Cook Webb, who was one of the child marchers, explained, "The reality of it is that we were born Black in Alabama, and we were going to get hurt if we *didn't* do something."

D-Day kicked off on the morning of May 2. Around 11:00, protest organizers arrived at campuses with signs saying, IT'S TIME! When the students spotted the message, they poured out of their schools. Some left the conventional way—through the front door—but others climbed through windows. "At one school, the principal gave orders to lock the gates to keep the students

They filled the church with the energy and enthusiasm that the movement desperately needed.

in," King later said. "The youngsters climbed over the gates and ran toward freedom."

About one thousand young people—aged from seven to eighteen—skipped school and converged on Sixteenth Street Baptist Church, where the mass meetings were held. "We poured into Sixteenth Street like a waterfall!" Webb recalled.

They filled the church with the energy and enthusiasm that the movement desperately needed. They laughed and smiled and sang and clapped as they waited for further instructions. Some of the children also helped make picket signs with messages that read, SEGREGATION IS A SIN, and I'LL DIE TO MAKE THIS LAND MY HOME.

Adults organized the young people into groups of fifty, and around noontime, Bevel instructed one group at a time to walk toward City Hall and the downtown business district.

Soon after the children left the church, police officers arrested them and hauled them to jail in paddy wagons or on buses.

Some of the children were able to avoid immediate arrest. Twelve-year-old Freeman Hrabowski joined one

Thousands of students were arrested during the Children's Crusade in Birmingham, Alabama.

of the breakaway groups, and though he was not the best singer, he belted out freedom songs led by others:

> Ain't gonna let nobody turn me around
> Turn me around, turn me around
> Ain't gonna let nobody turn me around
> I'm gonna keep on a-walkin', keep on a-talkin'
> Marchin' down to freedom land.

Hrabowski and his group made it all the way to City Hall, where they were to kneel and pray for freedom and tell anyone present that they were there to secure their rights.

Bull Connor was also at City Hall, and he was furious. With knees shaking, Hrabowski informed Connor that the group wanted to kneel and pray.

Connor spit in his face.

Before the end of the day, Hrabowski and about 970 other students had been arrested and were being held inside Birmingham's jails and juvenile detention centers.

That evening, worried parents surrounded Dr. King as he entered Sixteenth Street Baptist Church for the mass meeting. They wanted to know what he was going to do about the jailed children. "Are they okay?" they asked. "Will they be safe?" King remained calm and did his best to assure the parents that their children would be fine.

On May 3—the second day of the protest—thousands of young people gathered at the church and then at Kelly Ingram Park, a public park separating the Black sections of Birmingham from the white downtown area. The young people sang freedom songs and clapped and danced. About three thousand spectators came to the church to see the protest for themselves.

Bull Connor and his police force did not use violence against the young people on the first day of the protest, but that was about to change. Connor had positioned his force, as well as firefighters, at the public park. With the jails overflowing, he instructed the firefighters to turn their hoses on the young people.

The firefighters had supercharged the hoses, and the jets of water were so powerful that they blasted the young people off their feet, leaving them battered and bruised. Connor also ordered his force to turn their snarling dogs on the young people.

More than 1,900 children were arrested on the second day. The police used school buses to haul students to the pigpens at the city fairgrounds. The stench was so bad that many of the young people began to feel ill.

Newspapers from around the world, as well as television news programs, showed images of German shepherds attacking children, of firehoses knocking them off their feet, of little kids sitting in jail.

President John F. Kennedy said the images made him sick. They humiliated the United States on the global stage. American political leaders often spoke of the need for freedom in other countries, especially in the Soviet Union, but these images showed that Black people in the United States were also denied freedom.

Despite the horrific violence, thousands more young people showed up for the third day of protest. They returned to Kelly Ingram Park and faced off against police officers and firefighters. Yet again, thousands were arrested and sent to the fairgrounds or any place where the police could jail them.

Joining them in jail was the famous comedian Dick Gregory. Known for his civil rights work, Gregory was struck by the joy he encountered in his interactions with his jail mates. He was also amazed by their courage. He later shared a story about a four-year-old boy who told him 'teedom' was his reason for being jailed. "He couldn't even say *freedom*, man," Gregory remembered.

For some, being in jail for the cause of freedom was reason to celebrate. But for others, it was a scary time. Rats and roaches were common, and some of

A student protester staring down a gnarling German shepherd police dog.

the older inmates were unfriendly. The incarcerated young people received just one bologna sandwich per day. They also had to sit for interrogations, intense questioning from police officers. But most were proud to be in jail.

The protests continued. On May 5, thousands gathered at Memorial Park, just across the street from the main city jail, to show their support for the young people behind bars. And on May 6, more children were arrested as they gathered for a protest at Sixteenth Street Baptist Church.

At that evening's mass rally, King said, "Don't worry about your children. They're going to be all right." But he also made another point. "Don't hold them back if

Officers arresting Parker High School student Mattie Howard on the sixth day of the Children's Crusade.

they want to go to jail, for they are doing a job for all of America, and for all mankind."

That job continued the following day as Shuttlesworth led another massive march of young people. The marchers seemed fearless, and they were as defiant as ever, even as firefighters blasted them yet again with painful jets of water. Shuttlesworth ended up in the hospital with a badly bruised body.

President Kennedy and his team wanted a resolution to the crisis. They sent Burke Marshall, an attorney who worked on civil rights, to gather together the opposing parties for discussions and negotiations. Urged on by Marshall, King called the demonstrations to a halt.

The compromise did not call for total desegregation throughout the city, but it represented a solid start.

On May 10, Shuttlesworth and King announced their support for a compromise that included the following actions: the release of the thousands of young people still in jail; the removal of WHITES ONLY and BLACKS ONLY signs from drinking fountains and restrooms; the formation of a plan to desegregate lunch counters and offer better jobs for Black people, and the creation of a committee of Blacks and whites to monitor the progress of the agreement. The compromise did not call for total desegregation throughout the city, but it represented a solid start.

White segregationists detested the compromise, and on the night that it was announced, they bombed the black-owned hotel where King had previously stayed. The explosion injured three people. The next night, the segregationists bombed the home of the Reverend A.D. King, Martin Luther King's younger brother. On May 12, President Kennedy sent US troops to military bases near Birmingham, with a promise to use them should the attacks continue.

The violence stopped for a while, but the segregationists continued to act against Black people. On May 20, the Birmingham Board of Education expelled more than 1,100 students who had been arrested during the demonstration. Three days later, a federal judge over-ruled that decision, and the victorious students headed back to class.

Still, the segregationists would not surrender. On June 11, Alabama Governor George Wallace, standing at the door of the university's main building, person-ally prevented two Black students from enrolling at the University of Alabama.

That evening, President Kennedy appeared on tele-vision to call for new civil rights laws. "The heart of the question is whether all Americans are to be afforded equal rights and equal opportunities, whether we are going to treat our fellow Americans as we want to be treated," he said. "Now the time has come for this Nation to fulfill its promise . . . I am, therefore, asking the Congress to enact legislation giving all Americans the right to be served in facilities which are open to the public—hotels, restaurants, theaters, retail stores, and similar establishments . . . I am also asking the Congress to authorize the Federal Government to participate more fully in lawsuits designed to end segregation in public education."

The president concluded with words about the young people in Birmingham. "They are acting not out of a sense of legal duty but out of a sense of human decency," he said. "Like our soldiers and sailors in all parts of the world they are meeting freedom's challenge on the firing line, and I salute them for their honor and their courage."

A protester holding her handmade sign while an officer confiscates others.

Tears flowed down King's face as he heard President Kennedy deliver this speech. "Looking back," King later wrote, "it is clear that the introduction of Birmingham's children into the campaign was one of the wisest moves we made. It brought a new impact to the crusade, and the impetus that we needed to win the struggle."

The struggle for first-class citizenship was far from over, but the children had made it possible to see a way forward. O

CHAPTER FIVE

The March on Washington for Jobs and Freedom

1963

By the time the march was to begin,
about 250,000 people had gathered

1960   1965   1970

On the morning of August 28, 1963, Bayard Rustin strolled over to the Washington Monument, where the March on Washington for Jobs and Freedom would officially begin around noon. He wanted to see the early results of eight weeks of intense planning.

Rustin grew worried as he surveyed the area around 6:00 a.m. Only a couple hundred marchers had arrived, hardly a good sign. When members of the press asked him where all the people were, he pulled a sheet of paper out of his pocket, checked his watch, and said, "Gentlemen, everything is going exactly according to plan." Only Rustin knew that the paper was blank.

This was the third national march on Washington organized by Rustin and his mentor, labor leader A. Phillip Randolph. The first occurred on October 15, 1958, when ten thousand young people, with Jackie Robinson leading the way, demonstrated for integrated schools. The march on Washington was so successful in attracting young people that Rustin and Randolph organized a second one to take place on April 18, 1959. This time, twenty-five thousand young people took to the streets in the nation's capital. Many of them shouted, "Five, six, seven, eight! These United States must integrate!"

In late 1962, Rustin and Randolph began imagining another march on Washington. Unlike the marches for

David Robinson marched with his famous
father, Jackie, the first Black player in Major
League Baseball in the twentieth century.

integrated schools, this one would address the dire eco-
nomic conditions suffered by many Black Americans,
especially the lack of jobs.

When they watched the young people in Birmingham
facing off with violent police officers and firefighters,
Ruskin and Randolph broadened the focus of their
march. It would be a march for jobs *and* freedom.

They approached leaders of the major civil rights
organizations. Although some were initially hesitant
to sign on, all of them did. Known as the "Big Six,"
the group included Randolph, Martin Luther King
Jr. of the Southern Christian Leadership Conference
(SCLC), Roy Wilkins of the National Association for the
Advancement of Colored People (NAACP), John Lewis
of the Student Nonviolent Coordinating Committee
(SNCC), Whitney Young of the National Urban League

(NUL), and James Farmer of the Congress of Racial Equality (CORE).

The next two months were unbelievably busy. Rustin used index cards for planning, and he printed flyers and posters to spread the word. Telephones rang constantly, with people requesting information, reporters seeking interviews, and civil rights leaders determining their roles.

Marchers were instructed to bring peanut butter sandwiches, apples, cakes, and soft drinks—items that wouldn't spoil in the hot August sun. Three hundred volunteers also used five tons of American cheese to prepare eighty thousand sandwiches for sack lunches. Giant water tanks would supply twenty-one temporary water stations.

Rustin and his assistants also enlisted two hundred volunteer nurses and doctors to work at twenty-five first-aid stations. No detail was too small, including deciding on the number of portable toilets needed for the day—two hundred.

Seventeen-year-old Sondra Michelle Barrett was excited when she heard about the march, and she volunteered to serve as one of the thousands of marshals in charge of crowd control. A lifelong resident of Washington, DC, Barrett was personally familiar with racial injustice. During her elementary school years, she was prohibited from attending the school across the street from her house. Although named for a famous Black poet, Phillis Wheatley Elementary was for white students only.

Barrett wasn't allowed to play on the playground, either, even when school was not in session. Nor was she able to enjoy the nearby amusement center at Glen Echo Park, with its carousel, roller coasters, bumper cars, and massive swimming pool. Barrett was five or six years old when she learned that the park was for white kids only. She was so angry, she and her sister wrote and circulated a protest petition addressed to President Dwight Eisenhower. The girls secured several signatures from their neighbors before mailing the petition to the White House. President Eisenhower did not write back.

But the *Brown v. Board of Education* decision of 1954 changed Barrett's life. She was now permitted to attend Wheatley Elementary and to play on its playground.

Barrett attended integrated schools for the remainder of her public education. One of the things that shocked her at the new school was that the white kids were not the geniuses she'd imagined them to be. In the early 1960s, she attended Western High School in the Georgetown section of Washington, where she discovered a group of kids who were politically active. Barrett joined the High School Students for Better Education, which protested against a "tracking system" that unfairly placed Black kids in a curriculum that did not allow them to take college-preparatory classes.

Barrett was five or six years old when she learned that the park was for white kids only.

She also joined the Nonviolent Action Group (NAG), a protest organization founded at Howard University, where her sister was a student. Barrett and an integrated group of high school friends, all of them members of NAG, visited restaurants in nearby Virginia to see whether the waitstaff would serve Black people. These were not sit-ins. Rather, they were designed to gather facts that other civil rights groups would then use for later protests.

Barrett was a full-fledged activist by the time she learned about the March on Washington for Jobs and Freedom, and she was looking forward to taking part. During the run-up to the march, she and other NAG members were planning to carry out additional nonviolent protests during the event. "We were going to shut down the city," Barrett recalls. "We were going to lay our bodies on the bridges." But those radical plans were set aside when adult civil rights leaders encouraged everyone, for the sake of unity, to focus on the more moderate tactics of marching and rallying.

Barrett signed up to be a volunteer marshal who would help with crowd control. She was assigned a city block, and part of her job was to escort people from her block to the marshal at the next one.

Meanwhile, longtime segregationist Senator Strom Thurmond of South Carolina tried to derail the march by publicizing information about Rustin's past arrest and his affiliation with communists. Reporters asked Randolph, the official director, if he intended to ask Rustin to resign. "No," Randolph replied. "Rustin is Mr. March-on-Washington himself." Rustin kept his job; Thurmond lost his battle. The march was unstoppable.

On the day of the march, Rustin's early-morning worries soon disappeared. By 9:30 a.m., 40,000

Neighborhood kids on Capitol Hill offering free lemonade to marchers.

The group of marchers was interracial and intergenerational.

people were ready to go. Ninety minutes later, there were 90,000. The people kept coming, and the excitement kept building. By the time the march was to begin, about 250,000 people had gathered.

The official march would start at the foot of the Washington Monument, about a mile from the Lincoln Memorial, where an afternoon program would take place. There was a stage at the Washington Monument, and before the march began, blues artist Josh White sang the lyrics beloved by Birmingham's young marchers: "Ain't nobody gonna stop me, nobody gonna keep me, from marchin' down freedom's road." Celebrities and athletes also appeared onstage to empower and motivate the crowd. Perhaps the most famous celebrity was Jackie Robinson, who had broken the color barrier in Major League Baseball when he debuted with the Brooklyn Dodgers on April 15, 1947.

Students in their school uniforms marching down Constitution Avenue.

Jackie and Rachel Robinson had brought along their three children: Jackie Jr., Sharon, and David. Of the three, thirteen-year-old Sharon was the most anxious about the day. She had watched the Birmingham officials turn hoses and dogs on Black students, and she worried the same might happen to her.

Jackie was on stage at the Washington Monument because he was scheduled to welcome everyone to the march. Sharon was still feeling a bit anxious, but she was thrilled to see her father standing next to Martin Luther King Jr. When Jackie moved to the podium, the crowd erupted in applause. The hall-of-famer welcomed the marchers and told them that he and Rachel and their three children would be joining them. "I know all of us are going to go away feeling we cannot turn back," he said. Again, the crowd cheered.

The march to the Lincoln Memorial began around noon. Thousands of children, young people, and adults made the one-mile walk. Some were holding signs that read, WE MARCH FOR INTEGRATED SCHOOLS NOW!; WE MARCH FOR JOBS FOR ALL NOW!; WE DEMAND AN END TO BIAS NOW!; and WE DEMAND DECENT HOUSING NOW!

The heat and excitement proved too much for Sharon. She fainted. Her mother Rachel took her to a first-aid tent, and after drinking some fortified water and eating a pack of peanut butter crackers, she made it to the Lincoln Memorial in time for the speeches.

The official program started at 2:00 p.m. Marian Anderson, a Black opera star, sang the national anthem, and A. Phillip Randolph welcomed everyone. As the main organizer, Rustin buzzed about like a stage manager, making sure everyone was on time, in place, and had their speeches ready.

John Lewis—the twenty-three-year-old SNCC president—delivered the most militant speech of the day: "I appeal to all of you to get into this great revolution that is sweeping this nation," he said. "Get in and stay in the streets of every city, every village and hamlet of this nation until true freedom comes, until the revolution of 1776 is complete. We must get in this revolution and complete the revolution."

Black student leader John Lewis, fifth from left, gave the most militant speech of the day.

Sondra Barrett could not hear Lewis's speech from where she was stationed. She couldn't hear any of the speeches. Barrett was far from the steps of the Lincoln Memorial, where the speakers were located, and the sound system wasn't powerful enough to reach her. "That was a real, real disappointment for me," she recalls. "But I had a job to do, and I took my job seriously."

Barrett missed the speeches, but she was shocked and thrilled when a major Black civil rights leader walked into her assigned area.

Malcolm X was a famous minister in the Nation of Islam—a Black religious group founded by the Prophet Elijah Muhammad—and he was the main representative of Black nationalism in the United States. Unlike Martin

Twelve-year-old Edith Lee holding her souvenir banner.

Luther King Jr., Malcolm X did not believe in racial integration. He maintained that Black people would not be free until they possessed and occupied their own land independent from white society, and ran their own schools, businesses, and institutions. Further, unlike King, Malcolm X was not a pacifist. He believed that Black people had the right to use "any means necessary," including physical force, when defending themselves.

When she was younger, Barrett had been afraid of the militant leader. "I was afraid of him because I was an integrationist, and I was kind of a pacifist, and he was saying, 'by any means necessary.' And I was like, 'Oh, no.'" But Barrett had developed deep respect for Malcolm X. She had heard him debate Rustin at

Howard University a few years before the march, and she admired the skilled way he argued.

Barrett did not have the chance to speak one-on-one with Malcolm at the march. Although she escorted him, he was surrounded by members of the media and his colleagues in the Nation of Islam. But the moment had a powerful effect on her. "He just knocked me out," she said. "I felt I was in the presence of genius, that I was in the presence of greatness."

Back on stage, the speeches continued. Rustin had scheduled King to be last, because he knew that the Baptist preacher from Atlanta was the most influential voice in the civil rights movement. As the final speaker, King would give the march its exclamation point.

King strode to the podium and began to speak. He started off slowly, and at first, his speech did not seem like anything special. But then he silenced the 250,000 marchers, holding them spellbound, as he began to share his powerful dream for the nation.

"I have a dream," he said. "I have a dream that . . . one day right there in Alabama, little Black boys and Black girls will be able to join hands with little white boys and little white girls as sisters and brothers. I have a dream today!"

As she listened to King deliver his speech, Sharon Robinson thought of the time when students in her

Marchers often clapped, sang, and chanted on their way to the Lincoln Memorial.

elementary school had made prejudiced comments about her skin. But she also heard a more powerful message—that she had the right to stand up for herself, to speak up for herself, to be the person she wanted to be.

After King finished sharing his dream, the sea of people standing in front of the Lincoln Memorial erupted in applause, cheers, smiles, and tears. It was to become King's most famous speech and a defining moment in world history.

Then Rustin stepped to the podium to read the demands of the march. "Friends," he said, "at five o'clock today, the leaders whom you have heard will go to President Kennedy to carry the demands of this revolution."

The president was watching the march on television at the White House. Millions of citizens across the

Many young marchers traveled to the nation's capital with friends from home and school.

country also watched from the comfort of their homes. All major newspapers and radio stations covered the historic event.

"It is now time for you to act," Rustin continued. "I will read each demand and you will respond to it." As he read the demands, he punctuated his words by thrusting his right arm into the air.

"The first demand," he announced, "is that we have effective civil rights legislation, no compromise . . . and that it include public accommodations, decent housing, integrated education . . . and the right to vote. What do you say?" The crowd roared its approval.

After the march, the civil rights leaders visited President Kennedy at the White House. Lewis recalls, "He

Kennedy did not submit new legislation.

stood in the door of the Oval Office, and he greeted each one of us. He was like a beaming, proud father. He was so pleased. So happy that everything had gone so well."

Kennedy was pleased that no violence had occurred, but there was still some tension during the meeting. The march leaders told the president that they wanted a stronger civil rights bill than the one he had introduced. They wanted legislation that addressed all the demands approved by the marchers.

Kennedy did not submit new legislation. He was assassinated three months after the march. But in the following year, with strong support from President Lyndon Johnson, Kennedy's successor, Congress passed the Civil Rights Act of 1964. Martin Luther King Jr. attended the White House ceremony where Johnson signed the bill and made it the law of the land.

The peaceful marchers—including Sondra Barrett, Sharon Robinson, and thousands of other young people—had helped to persuade Congress to pass civil rights legislation.

The peaceful protesters also had helped to establish a record. The 1963 March on Washington for Jobs and Freedom was, so far, the largest and most important nonviolent protest for civil rights in US history. O

CHAPTER SIX

The Fight for Free Speech at School

1965
The march takes place on November 27, 1965

| 1960 | 1965 | 1970 |

In 1957, five-year-old Mary Beth Tinker accompanied her father and siblings to City Hall in Atlantic, Iowa. Her father, the Reverend Leonard Tinker, was a minister in the small town, and he wanted to show his children the importance of standing up for their beliefs.

Tinker, a white man, believed in racial equality, and he had recently discovered that the town prohibited its one Black family from using the public swimming pool. He rounded up his children, headed to City Hall, and demanded the town open the pool to everyone.

The demand fell flat. Atlantic's political leaders did not integrate the public pool. Tinker lost his job because his congregation did not support his belief in racial equality. A local church in Des Moines had invited him to become its minister, so the Tinker family moved. Unfortunately, like Atlantic, Des Moines was not an easy place for them to express their beliefs in peace, justice, and equality.

Her father's protests left an impression on Mary Beth. "I learned that this was the way to live—to stand up for what you believe in . . . that there would be risks."

Mary Beth, too, stood up for her beliefs. She was motivated partly by deep religious convictions: her parents had taught her about the importance of treating all people with respect and dignity, and about the pain and destruction caused by violence. Like her parents, Mary Beth believed in peace, and she wanted to share this with her classmates. In fourth grade, she wrote a speech on the possibility of peace, but her teacher said that the topic was too controversial for the classroom. Her teacher, like most people in the area, probably believed that war was sometimes required to protect the United States and its citizens. The school superintendent agreed with the teacher, and he denied Mary Beth permission to give the speech.

In the early 1960s, people who believed in peace turned their attention toward a war in Vietnam, a small country in Southeast Asia. The conflict pitted a pro-communist government in northern Vietnam against an anti-communist government in the South.

The United States opposed the spread of communism and sent troops to support the government in South Vietnam. Mary Beth and her family—who often discussed politics at the dinner table—did not support the US military's involvement in Vietnam. The Tinker kids were especially moved by news reports about the war. As Mary Beth recalls, "We would come home from school and watch the evening news and see images of burned villages, children crying, soldiers injured and dead." The Tinker family showed their opposition by going to local peace marches.

Like her parents, Mary Beth believed in peace, and she wanted to share this with her classmates.

In 1965, Mary Beth's older brother John, a high schooler, decided that he wanted to go to a peace march in Washington, DC. He had heard that a local Quaker and leader of a group of farmers for peace had chartered two buses to make the long trip from Des Moines to the nation's capital. Without stops, the trip would take about sixteen hours. Despite the distance, John was determined to ride, stand up, and march for his belief in peace.

John's parents agreed to let him go. His mother, Lorena, and his sister Bonnie, a student at nearby Grinnell College, would join him on the trip.

The two buses were filled mostly with farmers, college students, and local peace activists, including John's friend from his youth group, Christopher Eckhardt, and Christopher's mother Margaret Eckhardt, the president of the Des Moines chapter of the Women's International League for Peace and Freedom.

The March on Washington for Peace in Vietnam took place on November 27, 1965. The weather could not have been nicer. It was bright and sunny, with just a slight chill in the air.

... peace activists were planning to wear black armbands as a way of continuing the protest.

About twenty-five thousand protesters had arrived in Washington. At 11:00 a.m., they began to march around the White House. Picket signs popped up everywhere. Their messages included: STOP THE BOMBINGS; BRING THE TROOPS HOME NOW; and NEW ACTION TO SPEED NEGOTIATION.

After picketing for two hours, the protesters marched to the Washington Monument for a 2:00 p.m. rally. Among the keynote speakers that day was Martin Luther King Jr.'s widow, Coretta Scott King, who said, "Freedom and destiny in America are bound together with freedom and justice in Vietnam."

Long-time peace activist Norman Thomas told the crowd that if he were President Lyndon Johnson, he would declare: "I am the President of the most powerful nation in the world—therefore, I say this war will stop and I say we will stop the bombing."

John Tinker was captivated by the speeches, the march, the picketing—the entire event. As he recalled later, "The main impression of being in that crowd in DC was the realization of the vast numbers of people who thought that the US should not be in

Vietnam. I had never seen so many people together in one place."

But the most significant thing to happen to John that day was a conversation after the march. On the bus ride home, the organizer told his fellow riders that peace activists were planning to wear black armbands as a way of continuing the protest. John and Chris loved the idea and decided they would organize students to wear armbands to school.

To solidify the plan, the Eckhardt family hosted a meeting at their home on December 11. The students there decided to wear black armbands at school from December 16 to New Year's Day. They intended for the silent protest to symbolize their mourning for all of the victims of the war and to call for a Christmas truce.

About sixty students supported the silent protest; these included members of Liberal Religious Youth, the youth group that John and Chris attended at the Unitarian Universalist church. One of the members, Ross Peterson, wrote an article about the protest for the Roosevelt High School newspaper. Titled "We Mourn," the article never made it to print. The principal decided it was too controversial to publish, and even went so far as to inform nearby principals, as well as school district administrator E. Raymond Peterson, about the coming protest. In turn, they held a meeting and decided the schools would not allow the students to wear armbands. When contacted by the press, the district administrator said, "The schools are no place for demonstrations." He added that the ban was based on a standing policy

Mary Beth, third from right, at a civil rights protest years before she wore her armband to school.

against "anything that is a disturbing situation within the school."

On December 15, the *Des Moines Register* published a front-page story about the school district's ban. The students did not meet that night, but many who had planned to participate in the protest decided not to wear armbands. In all, only about a dozen students—including John, Mary Beth, and Chris—were still committed.

John and Mary Beth talked with their parents. Lorena offered her support right away, but their father hesitated. "We talked to him about our conscience, because my dad had always taught us to stand up for our conscience," Mary Beth said. The Tinker kids also asked their father to look at his own actions and the risks he had taken when he chose to stand up for his beliefs.

"Well," Mr. Tinker said, "I guess you're right. I have taught you to stand up for what you believe in."

Before school on December 16—the first day of the scheduled protest—John was delivering newspapers when he decided that they should call things off, at least until they had a chance to meet and discuss the ban. By the time he arrived back home, though, Mary Beth had already left for Warren G. Harding Junior High School—and she was wearing her armband. John got on the phone right away and called the other student protesters. They agreed with him, but Chris Eckhardt said he didn't care—he was going to wear the armband.

Mary Beth had pinned a one-inch strip of black cloth over her sweater. She had also taken a petition with her that stated that students should have the right to wear armbands, crucifixes, and other political and religious symbols.

"I was very nervous," she recalls. "It was kind of a moral dilemma because I didn't want to get in trouble. But there again I remembered these other young people, mostly from the civil rights movement, who had been brave, who had risked their lives, even lost their lives, to speak up for what they believed in."

Mary Beth walked into school. In her morning classes, the armband sparked several discussions about her protest. When her friend Connie said she thought Mary Beth should take it off before she got into trouble, Mary Beth explained, "Connie, I'm so sad about the war."

After lunch, Mary Beth had math class. Her math teacher had spent the previous day telling his students that anyone wearing an armband to his class would be in trouble. Shortly after Mary Beth took her seat, he sent her to go see the school counselor.

Waiting for the counselor, Mary Beth talked to the vice principal about her silent protest. She was still feeling nervous, and the vice principal told her that all she had to do was to take off the armband.

Mary Beth paused. She looked around the office. She looked at the vice principal. And then she took off her armband.

She thought the incident was over when he gave her a pass to return to math class. But ten minutes later, she was called back to the office. This time, she met with the counselor. As Mary Beth recounted, "She told me she was sorry, but she would have to suspend me. She said she had to follow orders, but she sympathized with my opinion. She told me she understood my point of view because her grandparents had been Quakers."

Suspended from school, Mary Beth went home.

Meanwhile, Chris Eckhardt was facing trouble at Roosevelt High School. Roosevelt's football coach had been encouraging his players to beat up opponents of the war, and on the way to school that morning, the captain of the football team had noticed Chris's armband and attempted to rip it off.

Chris decided that he would go to the principal's office as soon as he arrived at school. According to

DES MOINES PUBLIC SCHOOLS

NOTICE OF SUSPENSION

To Mr. and Mrs. Leonard E. Tinker   Date 65/12/16

Address 704 Grandview   Regarding: Mary Beth
                                     (Name of Pupil)

From Warren Harding Jr. High   Birth Date 65/9/8   Grade 8
     (School)

This is to inform you that Mary Beth
has been suspended from school because: she was wearing an arm band which the Board of
Education ruled out at their meeting this week.

It will be necessary for a parent or guardian to call Mrs. Tarman

of Warren Harding Jr. High   Telephone number 244-9189   244-9189
for an appointment.

c/c Mr. Pratt
    Mr. Cerwinske   (Signed)
                               (Principal) Girls' Adviser

Form 683 200 pads 6-64 D. M. Tech Press

Before her protest, Mary Beth had never been suspended from school.

101

Chris, "The counselor asked if I wanted to go to college, and said that colleges didn't accept protesters. The vice principal asked if I wanted a busted nose. He said seniors would not like the armband." The threats scared Chris, and tears welled up in his eyes.

The vice principal and counselor asked him to take off the armband. Chris refused. They asked again. Chris refused again. The vice principal then gave him a pass to go home as well as a notification that he would fail all of his classes that day. A suspension notice would soon be in the mail.

Later that afternoon, the student protesters held a meeting to discuss their next steps. They telephoned the school superintendent to see whether he might call an emergency board meeting so that the students could present their case. When the superintendent refused, John Tinker knew what he had to do: he would wear his armband to school.

On December 17, John put on some extra-nice clothes—a white shirt, tie, and sport coat. He didn't usually dress up for school, but he thought the professional outfit would help others understand that he wasn't trying to be disruptive or disrespectful.

John put the armband in his pocket. "I didn't want to wear it on the street," he explained. "I was a little concerned for my safety."

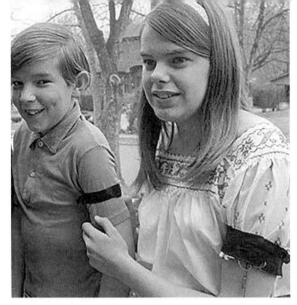

Mary Beth Tinker and her younger brother, Paul, wearing their anti-war armbands.

On the way out the door, his father stopped him.

"Are you sure you want to wear that armband?" Mr. Tinker asked. "The school made a rule, and maybe that's the way it should be."

"This is a piece of black cloth," John replied. "People are dying in Vietnam."

His father agreed, and John headed to school with the support of his parents.

After homeroom, John went to the restroom and tried to put on his armband. A student saw him struggling and offered his help. Together they pinned it onto John's sleeve. The black band left him feeling self-conscious. He was aware of how much attention was on him.

In the following class periods, some students asked him about the silent protest. Others warned him that he'd get in trouble. And still others made fun of him. At lunch, a group of kids came up to his table and called him names. "Pinko!" they shouted. "Commie!" These were shorthand words for *communist*. The students suggested that by opposing the war in general, John supported the communists on the other side of it. They continued to ridicule him until a large football player, Steve Kline, also came over to the table.

"Look," Kline said, "you have your opinion about the war. John has his opinion about the war, and John has a right to his opinion, so leave him alone."

After lunch, John headed to English class. As soon as he walked into the classroom, the teacher told him to go see the principal.

"I suppose you know I have to ask you to take it off," the principal said.

"Yes, I do," John said.

"I don't suppose you will."

"No."

The principal was cordial during the exchange. He asked John to share his reasons for protesting. He also told John that although he would not be suspended, he could not come back to school until the policy changed or John agreed to take off his armband. This was the same message given to all twelve students who had worn armbands to school.

John understood, and his father picked him up and drove him home.

Word about the protest spread quickly, and about two hundred people attended the regularly scheduled board meeting on December 21. By this point, the Tinker and Eckhardt families had asked for help from the Iowa Civil Liberties Union (ICLU), a group of lawyers and advocates devoted to protecting constitutional rights.

An ICLU attorney represented the students at the meeting. He said that the board had violated the students' right to free speech. He also asked that they end the ban and adopt a new policy allowing students to express their opinions at school. The board denied the request and voted to extend the ban. A few weeks later, they voted again, upholding the ban as official school policy.

The students returned to class after the holiday break, but only because they knew that the ICLU was now continuing their fight. Rather than wearing black armbands—which would have led to more suspensions—they wore black clothes for the remainder of the school year. They knew the school board couldn't ask them to take their clothes off!

On March 14, 1966, ICLU attorney Dan Johnston filed a federal lawsuit representing John and Mary Beth Tinker, Chris Eckhardt, and their fathers. The suit argued that the school board had violated the students' constitutional right to free speech.

The original armbands worn by Mary Beth and John did not include the peace sign.

This was not an easy time for John, Mary Beth, and Chris. They received hate mail and threatening phone calls. Chris's girlfriend broke up with him, and John was dunked and held under water in swimming class. Vandals splashed red paint, the color associated with communism, across the Tinkers' driveway. A radio show host even encouraged people to assault Mr. Tinker.

Eventually, the case ended up at the Supreme Court of the United States. On February 24, 1969, the Court ruled in favor of the students, with seven votes for them and two against. Justice Abe Fortas wrote the opinion for the majority. "In our system, state-operated schools may not be enclaves of totalitarianism," he stated. "School officials do not possess absolute authority over their students."

Fortas stressed that students had rights even during school time, writing, "It can hardly be argued that either students or teachers shed their constitutional rights to freedom of speech or expression at the schoolhouse gate."

Public schools were permitted to limit student protests if they infringed on the rights of others or created a substantial interference with school discipline. But otherwise, students were now free to protest at public schools.

Mary Beth, John, and Chris had won!

By the time of the ruling, John and Chris were in college. The Tinker family had left Des Moines and was now living in St. Louis. When Mary Beth heard the news, she was at home. "My mom went and got some ice cream and soda pop," Mary Beth recalled. "And we had a little celebration."

But the Tinkers weren't too happy. "It was a terrible year for the war—1969—and so we couldn't really rejoice. And also, we hadn't stopped the war. We were supposed to celebrate because we could wear little black armbands now? It didn't feel like such a great victory."

But Mary Beth eventually came to see that the case was truly historic. It cleared the way for millions of other students to stand up for their beliefs in the years to come. O

CHAPTER SEVEN

The Student Walkouts of East Los Angeles

1968
*Chicanx students in East
Los Angeles have had enough*

1960   1965   1970

"You little Mexicans," Patssi Valdez's white home economics teacher at Garfield High School in East Los Angeles said. "You'd better learn and pay attention. This class is very important because most of you are going to be cooking and cleaning for other people."

Paula Crisostomo had a similar experience at Lincoln High School, also in East Los Angeles. One day, she approached her geometry teacher to ask about an assignment, and he rolled his eyes, saying, "Oh, come on, Paula. We all know you're never going to college. You and your girlfriends back there are going to be pregnant by the end of the summer. Go and sit down. Don't waste my time." This insult, often thrown at women of color, played into the stereotype that Latinx women are less deserving of education and less capable of achievement.

Valdez and Crisostomo—like many other Chicanx students in East Los Angeles in 1968—felt as if their white teachers did not respect them as serious students with academic abilities.

In 1968, high schools in East Los Angeles—including Belmont, Garfield, Lincoln, Roosevelt, and Wilson—were failing to give a high-quality education to Chicanx

. . . many Chicanx students dropped out of high school before graduating.

students. About 75 percent of the students in these schools were Chicanxs, and their education was not equal to that of students in predominately white schools.

The East Los Angeles schools were in poor physical shape. Historian Ian F. Haney Lopéz describes them as "large dilapidated concrete buildings surrounded by stretches of crumbling pavement and high chain-link fences." The run-down buildings were packed with students. Some classrooms did not have enough chairs, and students had to sit on the floor. Lincoln needed more classrooms, more books, more paper, more teachers, and more counselors.

To make matters worse, Chicanx students had little choice about the track of their education. Most were placed in programs that focused on the industrial arts (such as carpentry) or family and consumer arts (such as cooking). Those who did plan to go to college were ill prepared by the time they graduated from high school.

Although most students spoke Spanish at home, they were prohibited from uttering a word of Spanish at school. If they were caught doing so, they were often ridiculed and expelled from class. When former student Harry Gamboa was in elementary school, his teacher asked him to come to the front of the class. He obliged, and his teacher helped him make a cone hat out of construction paper. Gamboa thought that making the hat was an art project, but his teacher placed the cone on his head, wrote *Spanish* on it, and said he could take it off only when he learned to speak English. Gamboa was humiliated.

Because of the poor education they received, as well as the personal indignities they suffered, many Chicanx students dropped out of high school before graduating. On average, Chicanx students in East Los Angeles received only eight years of education before dropping out. One former student, Henry Gutiérrez, explains that it's more accurate to say that the students didn't drop out as much as they were pushed out by a poor and prejudiced educational system. At Garfield, 57 percent of students left school before graduation; at Roosevelt, 45 percent; and at Lincoln, 39 percent. Those were among the highest rates in the nation.

By 1968, Chicanx students in East Los Angeles had had enough, and they rebelled against the school system that was failing them so badly. Some of them were inspired to act by one of their few Chicanx teachers, Sal Castro, whose classes on civics and history were popular at Lincoln High School. He made sure his courses included sections on Mexico, Mexican culture, the Spanish language, and the presence of Chicanxs throughout US history. His educational mission was to instill a sense of pride and respect among his Chicanx students.

Castro also acted as a mentor to students who wanted to protest the poor education they were receiving. He helped them organize a local chapter of the United Mexican American Students (UMAS), a citywide club begun by Chicanx college students devoted to creating better educational opportunities for their peers. He also helped them attend a summer leadership conference at Camp Hess Kramer in Malibu.

Students who participated in UMAS and Camp Kramer planned ways to fight against inequality in their education. The students drew inspiration not only from Castro but also from recent strikes by farmworkers in Southern California, and they enthusiastically rallied around the idea of school walkouts.

To prepare for the walkouts, they developed and distributed a survey that collected the opinions of Chicanx students about their schools. Students Vicki Castro and Paula Crisostomo then delivered the survey results to the school board. The document also listed student demands, including the addition of courses in Mexican American history, the hiring of more Chicanx teachers and counselors, instruction in both English and Spanish, and an end to corporal punishment.

The board ignored the demands. "They patted us on the back," says Moctesuma Esparza, who was a college student and UMAS member at the time. "And my recollection is that they literally just threw away the results of our survey."

Teacher Sal Castro speaking to Lincoln High
School students during the walkout.

The board's negative response fired the students
up and strengthened their resolve to protest for a better education. They created walkout committees at
Garfield, Lincoln, and Roosevelt high schools and
developed a detailed plan for consecutive walkouts,
taking place at each high school one by one.

Before they had a chance to enact their plan, Donald
Skinner, the principal at nearby Wilson High School,
canceled the student production of Neil Simon's play
Barefoot in the Park. He believed that the play's dia-
logue was too adult, or inappropriate, for Chicanx students. Although Wilson students did not have a walkout
committee, they knew about the planned protests at
the other schools and agreed to stage their own.

Protesters used graffiti to share their message.

On Friday, March 1, about three hundred students walked out of Wilson High School to protest the principal's decision. When the administration locked the doors to the main exit, the students found a way out through the auditorium. They also threw fruits and vegetables at teachers who sought to prevent them from leaving. Outside, they held a rally and a sit-in, saying they would not return to class until the principal let them stage the play.

The walkout at Wilson forced the committees at the other schools to consider accelerating and activating a unified plan for a series of walkouts. But before a decision had been made, student leaders at Garfield forged ahead. Just before lunch on Tuesday, March 5, a fire alarm went off, and Garfield student organizers ran through the hallways, pounding on classroom doors and yelling, "Walkout! Walkout!"

The teachers were stunned, and the students were gleeful. Some poured out of their classes right away, while others ran to the windows to see what was going on outside. Joseph Rodriquez, then a sophomore, recalled a supportive teacher who noticed his interest in the protest. "You're free to go," the teacher told him.

Rodriquez took off, joining hundreds of other protesters gathering at the school's entrance. Many of the students were thrusting their fists into the air and yelling, "¡Viva la revolución!" ("Long live the revolution!")

Mita Cuarón jumped on a car parked in front of the school. She had an orange traffic cone in her hands, and she used it as a megaphone. "Walkout!" she yelled. "Walkout!"

About 80 percent of the students walked out. Many of them marched in front of the school, holding picket signs that the strike committee had made earlier. The signs read, NO MORE FENCES; SMALLER CLASSES; STRIKE NOW; and WALK OUT NOW OR DROP OUT TOMORROW.

As the students chanted and marched with their picket signs, four fire trucks pulled up to the school. Someone had called in a bomb threat. At least thirty sheriff's deputies in riot gear also arrived and announced that the protest was an unlawful assembly. The officers grabbed Mita Cuarón under her arms and dragged her away from the main group. John Ortiz recalls seeing an officer hit a girl on the head with his billy club.

A few students grabbed glass soda bottles from a parked delivery truck and threw them at the aggressive officers. Two were arrested. The remainder continued to march and hold a sit-in in the street in front of the school. By 3:00 p.m., police officers had cleared the students from the area. In the following days, Garfield students continued their protest by holding rallies at nearby Atlantic Park.

That night, teacher Sal Castro consulted with the high school student leaders, and they all agreed that Lincoln would walk out at 10:00 a.m. the following day, March 6, and that Roosevelt would walk out two hours later.

After the meeting, high school and college students made colorful signs that read, WE ARE NOT "DIRTY MEXICANS"; CHICANO POWER; YA BASTA; EDUCACIÓN, JUSTICIA; EDUCATION, NOT ERADICATION; BROWN IS BEAUTIFUL; UNITE FOR BETTER SCHOOLS; and VIVA LA RAZA (Long live the race, or community).

Crisostomo, the walkout organizer at Lincoln, remembers that the atmosphere at her school was "absolutely tense" and "electric" as they prepared. The students were primed to go, but they were also frightened. As Bobby Verdugo recalled, "Man, we were scared to walk out of class because of the possible consequences. If anyone tells you they weren't scared, they are either lying or forgot a lot."

"But we were fed up, you know?" he added. "A year earlier, a teacher had said to me, 'Verdugo, you have three strikes against you: You're an underachiever, you're lazy, and you're Mexican.'" Verdugo was ready to protest.

On Wednesday, March 6, Crisostomo anxiously waited for the Lincoln walkout to begin. "I was scared, excited, nervous," she said.

Some teachers in East Los Angeles called students "dirty Mexicans."

Her mother had played an active role in the planning of the walkout and had told Crisostomo to meet her in front of the school, but even with her mother empowering her, Crisostomo was still feeling unsure. "What if I'm the only one who gets up to do this?" she asked herself. "Can I really do this?"

When the bell rang at 10:00 am, signaling the students to leave, some stood up and headed for the doors. College student and walkout organizer Moctesuma Esparza rushed into the school and ran through the hallways, yelling for the students to walk out.

Crisostomo left her classroom. "I was afraid to look behind me to see if anyone else was coming," she said. But before long, classroom doors around her flung open, and students began to pour into the hallways and dash toward the exits. "The roar of their footsteps, all coming down the stairwell where I was—that was exciting." About 90 percent of the students at Lincoln High School walked out.

Crisostomo met her mother just as they'd planned, and the two grabbed signs and marched around the school. Hundreds of others did the same, with many

About 90 percent of the students at Lincoln High School walked out.

of them chanting, "Schools, not jails!" and "Education, not eradication!"

An hour later, the students marched about ten blocks to Hazard Park. They continued to chant and raise their signs for all to see. Then they pressed on to the office of the board of education, where they planned to present their grievances and demands to Superintendent Stuart Stengel.

When Stengel came out to speak to the students, their boisterous chants overpowered his comments. Speaking on behalf of the protesters, Esparza demanded that the superintendent arrange for the students to meet with the board of education.

Back at Roosevelt High School, the walkout began earlier than planned. It had initially been set for noon, but the school principal called a morning assembly where he tried to calm the students and keep them in school. That did not happen. Student council president Robert Sánchez took control of the microphone, declared that the assembly was useless, and called for the students to walk out right then and there.

Roosevelt students poured out of the school in waves, but a major obstacle awaited them. When they arrived at

Activist Freddie Resendez standing on top of a car outside Lincoln High School.

A wall of sheriff's deputies at Garfield High School.

their school's chain-link fence, they discovered that the gate had been locked. The walkout was now a lock-in.

Some students scaled the fence, and UMAS organizers waiting outside cheered loudly when they made it to the other side. Others shook the fence and pushed it so hard that it seemed ready to fall. Still the gate stood.

Then, college student Vicki Castro, a graduate of Roosevelt, helped students tie one end of a gym rope to the fence and the other end to her car. Vicki hit the gas, the fence came crashing down, and the students escaped. About 60 percent of the student body walked out.

Trouble soon arrived. The principal had called the police for assistance, and they came in full riot gear. The officers beat the fleeing students. While shouting racial slurs, they shoved their billy clubs into students' stomachs, grabbed them by their necks, threw them to the ground, and kicked them. Some students fought back by pelting the officers with eggs and bottles.

It was an ugly scene, but it was not enough to force everyone to return to school. The students who escaped the police brutality marched to nearby Evergreen Park, carrying signs that read VIVA LA REVOLUCIÓN.

On Thursday, March 7, Belmont High School students held their own walkout. It had been difficult for them to sit by while the other schools staged their protests. But their time had come, and both Chicanx and white students were ready.

Police officers were waiting in the wings. As the walkout began, the officers stormed the hallways, using their clubs to hit any student seeking to leave. Shouts and screams filled the air, and students ran as fast as they could.

That night, Castro met with high school and college leaders, and together they agreed that all Eastside schools would walk out at 9:00 a.m. the following day. The leaders made more signs and called their friends to spread the word. Friday would be one big blowout.

The next morning students from across East Los Angeles—not just Chicanxs but also white and Black students—poured into the streets, grabbing protest signs and chanting. It was a rainy day, and the ink on the signs ran, making the words unreadable. Some students went home, but about eight hundred marched to Hazard Park.

The police were present, too, but this time, their presence was peaceful, directing traffic away from the marching students. One officer even asked Castro if he wanted a ride to the park. Castro was surprised, but he hopped on the hood of an unmarked police car and waved at students on the way to Hazard. "I felt like I was the grand marshal of the Rose Parade," he later wrote. "The kids didn't know it, but I was crying." He was so proud of them.

The rally at Hazard Park began around 11:00 a.m. Castro had brought a portable microphone, and student leaders used it to deliver passionate speeches in both English and Spanish, modeling the bilingual communication they wanted to use in their classrooms.

Once again, they demanded an opportunity to present their grievances to the entire school board.

Students lining up behind the chain-link fence at Roosevelt High School.

This demand was non-negotiable, they said. They also called for a boycott of all classes the next Monday.

Not all student leaders spoke. As Crisostomo remembers it, "At that time, the boys usually did the public speaking. They were literally 'the front men.'" The girls, on the other hand, had done much of the organizing.

Two school board members attended the rally, calling for the students to return to school. But the students would not give in until their demands had been met. US Representative Edward Roybal had flown in from Washington, DC, to speak with the students. The first thing he did was ask the police officers to leave the park. "We don't need the police here," he said. "We can take care of business ourselves." The students appreciated that, but criticized him later when he declined to send the letter of support they had requested.

By the end of the day, about twenty thousand students from about fifteen schools, of many different races, ethnicities, and backgrounds, and as young as junior high, had walked out to protest for a better education.

Although they insisted on remaining in charge of the protests, the students also recognized that building alliances with parents and political leaders would help their cause. On Sunday, March 10, supportive adults took part in a community-led rally backing the students. With help from Castro, the students also seized an opportunity to meet at the Los Angeles airport with US Senator Robert F. Kennedy, who was planning to run for president.

Kennedy shook everyone's hands and said he knew about—and supported—their demands. Then, as Crisostomo recalls, "He raised his fist and said, 'Chicano Power.'" The moment moved Crisostomo and the other students deeply.

Kennedy stayed and chatted with them for about an hour. He later sent the students a telegram that read: "I support fully and wholeheartedly your proposal and efforts to obtain better education for Mexican Americans. *Viva La Raza.*"

More good news came later in the afternoon when the students learned that the board of education, as well as the superintendent and deputy superintendent, had finally agreed to meet with them. The meeting would take place the next day at 3:00 p.m. at the board's downtown office.

The kids were thrilled.

By the end of the day, about twenty thousand students . . . had walked out to protest for a better education.

Hundreds of Chicanx students and parents showed up for Monday afternoon's board meeting. Roosevelt student body president Robert Sánchez spoke on their behalf. His speech was passionate and emphatic. After recounting the grievances, he informed the board members that the students would present their demands—but only at a school board meeting held at Lincoln High. They wanted the board to see what Lincoln looked like.

Then, Sanchez fainted.

But not really. He faked it so that he could emphasize how hard it had been for the students to suffer and protest the many indignities they encountered at school. It was a very dramatic performance.

Other students spoke, too, and although they were not as theatrical as Sanchez, they supported his grievances.

Ray Ceniceros, the head of the Garfield teachers, also spoke. "We feel disturbed and ashamed that these kids are carrying out our fight," he said. "Apparently we have been using the wrong weapons. These kids found a new weapon—a new monster—the walkout."

It took a few hours, but the board eventually agreed, by a vote of six to one, to hold a meeting at Lincoln. The

"He raised his fist and said, 'Chicano Power.'"

board also voted not to punish any student who had participated in the walkouts.

The students hoped victory was close at hand.

Schools remained empty while Castro and the students continued to meet, finalizing their list of demands.

At the same time, parents and community leaders came together to form the Educational Issues Coordinating Committee (EICC). The EICC stated that the kids had done remarkable work, and that it was now time for the adults to step up and carry out their mission.

Castro and the students distributed the list of thirty-six demands to community members shortly before the meeting. It included the following:

- Compulsory and bilingual education in all East Los Angeles schools.
- Teachers and administrators to receive training in learning Spanish and Mexican cultural heritage.
- Teachers and administrators who show any form of prejudice toward students, including

failure to recognize cultural traditions, will be transferred.

- Textbooks and curriculum should be revised to show Mexican contributions to society, to show injustices they have suffered, and to concentrate on Mexican folklore.
- Class size must be reduced so teachers can devote more time to individual students.
- Counselor-student ratios must be reduced, and counselors must speak Spanish and have a knowledge of Mexican cultural heritage.
- Corporal punishment, which is carried out only in East Los Angeles schools, should be abolished throughout the district.
- Cafeterias should have more Mexican dishes, and mothers should be hired as kitchen staff and allowed to help prepare the food.

On Tuesday, March 26, the school board held its promised meeting at Lincoln High School. The auditorium was packed with more than a thousand people. After the meeting was called to order, the students and their adult representatives from EICC placed their demands before the board. Cheers rang out from the audience, but the board members were critical, saying they lacked the funds to satisfy some of the demands. The crowd jeered.

The meeting ended after four hours of intense discussion between the board members, the students, and their adult advocates.

The board agreed to hire more bilingual personnel, reduce the number of students per class, and create sub-committees to review and address the other demands. They also reiterated their commitment to refrain from punishing anyone who had participated in the walkouts.

Some students walked out of the meeting, disgusted that only a few of their demands had been met, but others felt victorious. They had made the board listen to them, and now the EICC would continue to push for reform.

The students returned to school.

At the end of May, Sal Castro was arrested and charged with conspiracy. He was upset when he realized he wouldn't be able to fulfill his promise of chaperoning at the Lincoln prom.

Twelve other adults who had been leaders of the walkouts also found themselves jailed for the same crime. Mass protests followed, and everyone except Castro was soon released.

The civics teacher remained in jail until June 2, when he found out he no longer had a job. The school board had fired him. "I couldn't believe it," Castro said, shocked that he had been fired for helping students. Once again, the community held protests, and Castro was reinstated several months later, though not as a teacher at Lincoln.

Change came slowly to the East Los Angeles high schools. The most visible and immediate improvement happened outside the high schools entirely: the University of California, Los Angeles increased its enrollment of Chicanx students from 100 in 1968 to 1,900 in 1969.

Over time, Chicanx students also saw the development of bilingual education, the hiring of more Chicanx teachers and administrators, the inclusion of Mexican history and culture in the curriculum, and the addition of Mexican food in cafeterias. It would take decades before they gained full access to college preparatory classes.

By 2020, the dropout rates at East Los Angeles schools showed a marked improvement since 1968. Garfield's dropout rate fell 13 percent; Lincoln, 21 percent; and Roosevelt, 28 percent. Although these rates indicate that these schools have begun to deliver a better education to Chicanx students, they are still troubling when compared to largely white schools in wealthier areas of the city, which have a dropout rate of about 5 percent.

One of the most significant effects of the walkouts is something that has endured: the sense among Chicanxs that they are a political force that can create positive change in their communities and in wider society and culture. The Chicanx students of East Los Angeles in 1968 created a lasting legacy that we still call "Chicanx Power." O

CHAPTER EIGHT

The Children's Campaign for Nuclear Disarmament

1981
*The thirty-five-mile march
begins in the town of
Washington, Vermont*

1980　　　　　　　　1985　　　　　　　　1990

Nessa Rabin hoped for a world where people would not be hungry, where children would receive an excellent education, and where everyone would be safe from war. With this goal in mind, she sent President Ronald Reagan a letter:

Dear Mr. President:

I am a 12-year-old girl living in a small town in Vermont. My parents are bakers and in the summer we have a big garden. I love my life, but when I think about the world situation I get a horrible feeling. I feel like I don't want to have children because their children and grandchildren may be in danger of a nuclear war. As a child I do not think it is my business to have to think about such things.

But I disagree with your judgment about the budget. For one thing, poor people really do need money, as do schools. I think you should not have cut that. For another thing, I do not think that the defense budget needs one more cent. I have heard again and again that we have enough weapons to destroy every person on earth 13 times. Please don't be too proud to negotiate a plan with the Soviet Union to at least cut down on our human killing weapons.

Nessa Rabin

Plainfield

President Reagan did not reply, but Anne Higgins, the person in charge of his mail, sent Nessa a very short note. "Thank you for your message to President Reagan," she wrote. "No matter how busy his day may be, he is always pleased to hear from interested young Americans."

Nessa was not pleased. She felt the White House had dismissed her concerns.

Nessa and her fifteen-year-old sister, Hannah, had been sharing their fears of nuclear war with friends and pen pals they knew through their family: sisters Susan and Becky Dennison (15 and 11), sisters Solveig and Maria Schumann (19 and 14), and Alice Belenky (22).

"We keep in touch year-round with letters," Hannah explained to a newspaper reporter at the time. "We started writing how scared we felt about the nuclear arms situation and all decided we had to do something to get other kids involved." She made a similar point in another interview: "We were wondering whether we would be alive in 20 years. We just had to do something."

The friends decided to get together in Plainfield in mid-May 1981. "We had to get organized," Nessa stated. "Decide what our goals were and how to get in touch with kids."

At the May meeting, the friends formed a new group: the Children's Campaign for Nuclear Disarmament (CCND). The group created a plan to organize children across the nation to write letters protesting nuclear weapons. The children would address their letters to

"We were wondering whether we would be alive in 20 years."

President Reagan, and CCND would hold a public reading of each letter in Lafayette Park, just across the street from the White House. Then they would try to hand-deliver the letters.

With the plan in place, CCND began the nitty-gritty work required to make it happen. The first task was to spread news about the letter-writing campaign. How could they invite children far and wide to join them?

The group settled on two methods for spreading the word about their protest. The first was to ask peace organizations and leaders to print a notice in their newsletters on the CCND's behalf.

"We are children who fear for the future of our world," the notice read. "The United States and the Soviet Union are building more and more human-killing weapons, and every day the threat of nuclear war becomes greater. Our leaders are making decisions that affect us, as children, more than anyone else." The notice also emphasized the importance of the children's voices. "Most kids think they can do nothing about nuclear war. Each letter to President Reagan calling for nuclear disarmament can help make a difference. So write yours now and send it to us soon!"

"... we need everyone to unite together to try to stop the building of nuclear weapons."

The second method was a "chain letter" to children they knew, inviting them to participate in the campaign. The letter asked each recipient to make copies of the letter and forward it to three other kids, who would then make and send their own copies. And on it would go. "We must stop this [nuclear arms race]!" the letter read. "But we can't do it alone, and we need everyone to unite together to try to stop the building of nuclear weapons."

Monique Grodzki was thrilled when she received the chain letter in June. Grodzki was founder and president of the Children's Peace Committee in New York City, and she and her group had already presented a petition for world peace to United Nations Secretary-General Kurt Waldheim. "We received a lot of media coverage and the usual 'me too's' from our adults," she wrote in her reply to the CCND, "but as you see the superpowers are racing with each other to be better equipped to destroy all of mankind as well as his environment. But we cannot give up! If enough of us yell out in protest then they will just have to listen!"

By the first week of August, more than sixty-five letters had arrived at the Rabin home in Plainfield.

Hannah Rabin, left, and her sister, Nessa Rabin, were early leaders of the Children's Campaign for Nuclear Disarmament.

But CCND realized it needed many more to make a significant impact. The group sent out additional requests and mailed press releases to newspapers across the country. These announcements not only got the word out, but also led journalists to interview organizers and write articles about the campaign. In one of her interviews, Hannah explained the group's reasons for choosing a letter-writing campaign. "Kids can say things in a powerful and direct way," she said. "Nuclear war is a matter of life and death for everyone. Children can understand that as well as adults . . .

It's a matter of survival. It's not a complicated issue. It's simple."

Nessa added, "If we get enough people to write, how can President Reagan ignore us? If two thousand kids say they don't want to die, how can he just go watch a football game?"

Not long after these interviews, Hannah, Nessa, and their friends joined a three-day walk for nuclear disarmament. The thirty-five-mile march began in the town of Washington, Vermont, and concluded in Moscow, Vermont. The organizers billed the event as the "Washington-to-Moscow Walk for Nuclear Disarmament." The title referred not only to the two towns in Vermont but also to the two main political powers in the nuclear race, the US government in Washington, DC, and the Soviet government in Moscow, Russia.

On the last day of the walk, about 100 children affiliated with CCND joined about 1,400 other protesters outside the Vermont State House in Montpelier for a rally that called for an end to the nuclear arms race. The children sang a song for world peace on the State House steps. Hannah introduced the singers by sharing CCND's main message: "For all the kids in the world, [we have] an appeal—stop making nuclear weapons now." She also read aloud several letters to President Reagan written by children from Vermont.

Hannah Rabin, left, and other CCND activists protesting at the White House on October 18, 1981.

By the end of September, CCND had received almost 600 letters from kids in more than twenty-five states. "They are beautiful letters, scary, sad, but also full of life," the CCND organizers wrote in a mailing. But Nessa was not especially hopeful that CCND would secure an audience with the president. CCND had written the White House at the beginning of June with a request to meet with him, but, according to Nessa, a staff member had responded with "a very bland letter saying the president is too busy."

By mid-October, more than 2,800 letters from kids in thirty-eight states had arrived in CCND's mailbox.

Most of the young people who sent them were between the ages of six and sixteen.

In the last week of the campaign, about 300 letters were being delivered to the mailbox every day. Nessa organized them carefully so that none were lost or misplaced. She stored them in CCND's office—a corner of her family's kitchen.

About forty CCND members poured out of two large vans and a car just before 8:00 a.m. on Saturday, October 18. The group had secured a permit to read the letters on the sidewalk directly in front of the White House—the perfect location for their public protest—and they could not have been more excited.

Once outside, they formed themselves into four reading teams with three kids each. The reader stood in the middle, a helper on either side, and all three faced the White House. With a chill in the morning air, the four teams began reading the letters, all at the same time, at exactly 8:00 a.m.

Their voices sounded tense at first. They were a bit nervous. But as the sun's rays became stronger, and as the kids grew more comfortable exercising their right to petition the government, the nervousness ebbed.

Those not involved in reading the letters held homemade picket signs protesting nuclear weapons and war, with messages like, END THE NUCLEAR ARMS RACE NOW;

DON'T DESTROY THE ONLY WORLD; and I WANT TO LIVE. Other CCND members handed out leaflets to passersby and offered to speak with anyone interested in their protest.

Journalists and other members of the media came to watch. They paid close attention to the reading of the letters and reported on them.

Seven-year-old Dan Marcotte's letter read, "Dear President Reagan, I do not like war, but I do like your haircut and jellybeans. I do not like people getting killed by bombs."

Eleven-year-old Tanya Birenbaum had written that the arms race was "really stupid . . . like two babies who are fighting, one has five rocks to throw at the other, but the other only has four so he gets two more rocks so he has one more . . . So please try to stop the competition on who can make more weapons and who has more power to be able to kill everyone. Please try to understand my concern. Please care, that's the least you can do."

Another letter said, "No matter what country started a nuclear war, our whole world could go out like a light bulb, and there would be no one to turn it on."

As the public reading continued, the kids learned that Thelma Duggin, the White House staffer in charge of youth issues, would officially receive the letters at 1:00 p.m. Up to this point, CCND had no idea whether their letters would even get inside the White House, let alone anywhere near the president. The kids were delighted.

But just two minutes before 1:00 p.m., another White House representative came out to say that Duggin would not receive the letters after all. The stated reason was that there was a policy forbidding White House staff members from appearing at events when media was present. The kids felt deflated.

To make matters worse, the White House turned on the lawn sprinklers just after delivering the bad news. The sprinklers soaked the kids, their lunches, and their letters.

Still, CCND would not halt the public reading. They continued on until 5:30 p.m. They finished the protest with the reading of an antinuclear petition signed by one hundred students from California. But was there really no way they could get their letters into the White House before returning home?

They decided to call the White House switchboard and ask whether they might be able to deliver the letters directly to the mailroom. It was a last-resort measure, but to CCND's surprise, the White House granted the request. An official directed the kids to take the letters to a side door of the Eisenhower Executive Office Building, right next to the White House.

They decided to turn the action into a march or, as Hannah described it, "a big parade." The CCND members lined up single file, with the White House on their left. Some of the kids hoisted picket signs, and others held manila envelopes stuffed with letters. Hardly anyone was around to see them at this point, but that didn't matter. The CCND kids knew that what was most

Many parents brought their children to the nuclear disarmament rally in New York City's Central Park on June 12, 1982.

important was that they were fulfilling their promise to all the young people who had written letters. A CCND representative entered the side door and soon walked back outside with J.T. Buckler, a clerk in the White House mailroom. The kids erupted with applause and cheers. Finally, someone in the White House had acknowledged them and agreed to receive all 2,800 letters.

The cheering continued as Buckler personally ensured that each of the letters would be delivered

"It's a rotten thing not to care about the future. We are the future!"

to the White House mailroom. "He's not President Reagan," Hannah said, "but the letters got inside the White House . . . We feel we did really well. All the letters were read . . . We got national media coverage—some, not a lot."

The kids were exhausted and still disappointed that neither President Reagan nor anyone from his staff had personally received the letters and visited with them. As Nessa explained, "The White House's refusal to acknowledge us shows how little the government cares about the thousands of kids who took the time to put their thoughts on paper and send it to the President. It's a rotten thing not to care about the future. We are the future!"

To CCND's surprise, President Reagan sent a letter of apology a month after CCND's protest at the White House:

Dear Miss Rabin and Friends:

I'm sorry about the difficulties you experienced in trying to deliver the many letters to me on October 17. I can imagine how disappointed you were when the presentation fell through at the last minute, especially after all the effort you made to build support.

Believe me, no one in this country wants to prevent nuclear war as much as I do. We are working now to strengthen our defenses, which I think are essential to the preservation of peace. But even as we do that, we must begin to find ways to bring about verifiable reductions in armaments, so that neither the United States nor the Soviet Union will represent a threat to the other. I have repeatedly pledged my best efforts to the achievement of that goal. You are not alone in your wish that all children, in all lands, may grow up free from the threat of war.

A few days later, CCND issued a public statement about President Reagan's apology. The statement quoted from the president's letter and then offered the following commentary:

We appreciate the President's letter, because it opens communication between the Children's Campaign and the White House. It is very important for the government to listen to the people, and finally the children's voices have been heard.

However, the Children's Campaign does not agree with the President's belief that the United States must strengthen our military to provide national security. The whole world has never been so insecure as it is now with the capability to destroy so much. *In a nuclear war there would be no winners and few survivors.*

We believe that the only way all the people, all the children, will be safe from a nuclear holocaust is for

the United States and the Soviet Union to stop building
nuclear bombs and take apart the ones which are
already built. *We must have total worldwide nuclear
disarmament immediately.*

Hannah Rabin felt a bit down after the trip to
Washington. "It's depressing to go to Washington,
to tell you the truth, because nothing happens," she
explained. "It feels like you're not being effective." Their
protest had not changed President Reagan's mind
about building nuclear weapons.

As Hannah and others were feeling defeated, additional letters from young people protesting nuclear
weapons poured into the CCND. Tens of letters turned
into hundreds, and hundreds turned into a thousand.
With renewed energy, the group announced that it
would go back to the White House for another public
reading in June 1982.

Before returning to Washington, they wrote an educational pamphlet titled *The Nuclear Threat—What
Kids Can Do.* The committee mailed the pamphlet to
several dozen other CCND groups that were beginning
to pop up across the country, asking each of the groups
to educate children in their own communities.

On June 12, 1982, the CCND helped to lead about
seven hundred thousand protesters in New York City,
in what would become the largest antinuclear march
and rally in US history.

A week later, about thirty CCND members returned
to the White House for another public reading. This

The CCND banner, upper right, raised high at the nuclear disarmament march in New York City.

time they had over 5,400 letters. They had also earned enough respect to warrant a face-to-face meeting with Thelma Duggin. Led by the Rabin sisters, the young activists relayed their message to Duggin that the government must stop building nuclear weapons and start dismantling those in existence.

It didn't work. CCND never convinced President Reagan to stop the nuclear arms race. But this does not mean that they failed. They educated thousands of children about the threat of nuclear war. They inspired thousands of children to protest. They gave voice to thousands of children who wanted to make sure that the future would exist. And they showed adults that children could do all this with or without them. ○

145

PART TWO

The Twenty-first Century

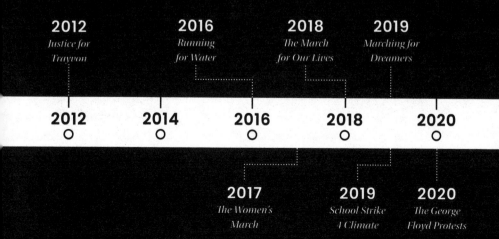

2012
Justice for Trayvon

2016
Running for Water

2018
The March for Our Lives

2019
Marching for Dreamers

2012 ○   2014 ○   2016 ○   2018 ○   2020 ○

2017
The Women's March

2019
School Strike 4 Climate

2020
The George Floyd Protests

CHAPTER NINE

Justice for Trayvon

2012
*George Zimmerman
kills Trayvon Martin*

2010   2015   2020

On the night of February 26, 2012, seventeen-year-old Trayvon Martin headed toward a 7-Eleven near his father's fiancée's house. After purchasing a bag of Skittles and some Arizona watermelon fruit juice, Martin strolled back to the house.

George Zimmerman, a twenty-nine-year-old neighborhood watch volunteer, spotted Martin walking back through the gated community. He saw the Black youth as a threat, and he called 9-1-1.

"Hey," Zimmerman told the police dispatcher, "we've had some break-ins in my neighborhood, and there's a real suspicious guy . . . This guy looks like he's up to no good, or he's on drugs or something. It's raining, and he's just walking around, looking about."

Zimmerman also stated that Martin was wearing a "dark hoodie" and moving toward him. But Martin then took off running, according to Zimmerman.

"Are you following him?" the dispatcher asked.

"Yeah," Zimmerman said.

"Okay, we don't need you to do that," the dispatcher replied.

Zimmerman asked for the police to call him when they arrived. After hanging up, he crossed paths with Martin. Zimmerman was armed with a semiautomatic pistol.

By the time the police arrived, Trayvon Martin was dead. He had been shot.

The Sanford Police Department believed that it did not have enough evidence to charge Zimmerman with a crime.

Zimmerman told officer Timothy Smith that he had shot Martin. Smith took Zimmerman's weapon. He later wrote that Zimmerman's back appeared to be wet and covered in grass, and that he was bleeding from the nose and the back of his head. The officers drove Zimmerman to the Sanford Police Department to interview him about the details of the killing.

During the interview, Zimmerman stated that "something was off" about Martin, and that he followed the Black youth first in his SUV and then on foot. Zimmerman also claimed that while he was chasing Martin, the teenager jumped in front of him, punched him in the face, knocked him down, and bashed his head into the cement. As Martin was beating him, he said, Zimmerman cried out for help and then shot Martin when it appeared that Martin was trying to grab Zimmerman's gun.

Zimmerman claimed the shooting was an act of self-defense.

Detective Chris Serino—who was conducting the interview—expressed skepticism about Zimmerman's

Trayvon Martin.

account. Why did Zimmerman believe that Martin was suspicious and that he was on drugs?

"Did it ever occur to you to ask this person what he was doing out there?" Serino asked.

"No, sir," Zimmerman replied.

"Do you think he was scared—do you think he thought you were trying to hurt him?" asked another police interviewer. "Can you see how this might frighten him?"

"I didn't have the opportunity," Zimmerman replied.

The officers also wondered why Zimmerman wasn't more badly injured, given what he claimed about the severity of Martin's attack.

The Sanford Police Department believed that it did not have enough evidence to charge Zimmerman with a crime. The shooter was free to go home.

Almost two weeks after the shooting, Trayvon's parents, Tracy Martin and Sybrina Fulton, created a petition asking for the local state attorney "to investigate my son's murder and prosecute George Zimmerman for the shooting and killing of Trayvon Martin."

On March 21, with no arrest on the horizon, about five thousand protesters, including hundreds of young students, converged on Union Square in Manhattan to demand Zimmerman's arrest. Many of the protesters wore hoodies, and they called the march the Million Hoodie March, to highlight that racist white people too often identify young Black people as threatening because of their clothing.

Tracy Martin and Sybrina Fulton spoke at the rally.

"I just want you to know that we're not gonna stop until we get justice for Trayvon," Martin said.

"Our son is your son," Fulton added. "I want you guys to stand up for justice and stand up for what's right. This is not a black-and-white thing. This is about a right-and-wrong thing. Justice for Trayvon!"

The crowd yelled back: "Justice for Trayvon! Justice for Trayvon! Justice for Trayvon!"

The rally then broke into three different marches. Some people headed downtown, while others headed uptown. A young boy wearing a hoodie held a sign that read, SKITTLES + ICED TEA = THREAT TO SOCIETY? Another Black boy with a hoodie carried a sign reading, DO I LOOK SUSPICIOUS? Still another held a sign: WILL I BE NEXT?

"I just want you to know that we're not gonna stop until we get justice for Trayvon."

Together, the marchers yelled, "We Are! Trayvon Martin!" and "We Want Arrests!"

The next day, Thursday, March 22, hundreds of students at Miami Carol City Senior High School—where Trayvon had attended as a freshman and sophomore—held a walkout. Unlike many protests with detailed planning, this one was spontaneous. Student leaders decided to walk out around 11:00 a.m. and then spread the word via Twitter, Facebook, and other social media. The walkout began at 12:30 p.m.

The principal gave his permission for a peaceful protest to take place on school grounds. Outside, the students held signs and chanted, "Justice for Trayvon!"

Several girls held a paper banner, signed by many students, that read, JUSTICE FOR TRAYVON MARTIN. One of the girls said that the banner was for Martin's family. She spoke directly to the family during an interview.

Student leaders decided to walkout around 11:00 a.m. and then spread the word via Twitter, Facebook, and other social media.

"This is for you," she said. "We are here for you. We're here for everything. We send our condolences from Miami Carol City High School."

Before long, students left campus and marched down Miami Gardens Drive, the town's main street near the school. Some students popped into nearby convenience stores to buy Skittles and iced tea in tribute to Trayvon.

The marchers took over the streets, grinding traffic to a halt. Along the way, they chanted, "Trayvon! Martin!" Some held paper hearts with Trayvon's name written in the middle. Others thrust their fists in the air.

Police officers were present, but they focused on keeping the students safe as they marched about a mile to a recreation center. Although the principal had not condoned the march, he helped to arrange for school buses to pick the students up and return them to school.

By the end of the day, more than one million people had signed the petition begun by Martin's parents.

Honoring Trayvon Martin at a memorial near the location of his death.

On Friday, March 23, President Barack Obama weighed in on the shooting. "I can only imagine what these parents are going through," he said. "Every parent in America should be able to understand why it is absolutely imperative that we investigate every aspect of this and that everybody pulls together—federal, state and local—to figure out exactly how this tragedy happened."

"If I had a son," the president added, "he'd look like Trayvon."

That morning, students from at least fifteen high schools and middle schools in the Miami area walked out of their classrooms. The number of protesters from each school ranged from 100 to more than 1,000. Some

Students from across the country, including these from Milwaukee, held marches and rallies calling for justice for Trayvon Martin.

marched off campus, while others stayed on school grounds. Students at Miami Southridge Senior High School in Cutler Bay streamed onto the football field and used their bodies to spell *TM*.

During the walkouts and marches, students expressed anger that Zimmerman hadn't been prosecuted. Black student protesters also shared their fear that their lives, too, were in danger. Melissah Debreus spoke for many when she said, "It could have been me."

Students at Dr. Michael M. Krop Senior High School—where Martin had attended as a junior—held a rally that turned into a march. It was not a planned protest, but it turned out to be a loud one as the students chanted, "What do we want? Justice! For who? Trayvon!"

Eventually, on April 11, Florida State's Attorney Angela Corey charged Zimmerman with second-degree murder, but the case was difficult partly because there were no witnesses. Corey's team failed to prove to the jurors that Zimmerman racially profiled Martin as a criminal, and that he intentionally and deliberately murdered the unarmed young man.

On July 13, 2013, a jury found Zimmerman not guilty. Protests immediately erupted across the country. A week later, an organized nationwide demonstration also took place, with rallies and marches in dozens of cities.

Tracy Martin spoke at a rally in Miami. "This could be any one of our children," he said. "Our mission now is to make sure that this doesn't happen to your child."

Sixteen-year-old Isabel Eugene was also at the Miami rally, and she emphasized that the shooting made Black kids terrified of the dangers they faced. "Before Trayvon, we took precautions, but now it's worse," she said. "It could have been my brother."

Sybrina Fulton spoke at a rally attended by thousands in New York City. "Trayvon was a child, and I think sometimes it gets lost in the shuffle, because as I sat in the courtroom, it made me think that they were talking about another man," she said. "And it wasn't. It was a child."

Fulton also offered a warning. "Today it was my son," she said. "Tomorrow it might be yours."

The Reverend Markel Hutchins, who helped organize the New York City protest, added a word of hope. "There's a new level of enthusiasm that I personally

A movement was indeed taking off.

have not seen since the days of the civil rights movement," he observed. "Perhaps Trayvon Martin's death—and perhaps even the not guilty verdict in the George Zimmerman trial—has inspired and ignited a movement of people who, frankly, needed to be moved."

A movement was indeed taking off.

Right after the announcement of the Zimmerman verdict, Alicia Garza, a young Black woman from Oakland, California, came up with the phrase *Black lives matter*. She typed what she called a "love letter to Black people" and posted it on Facebook. The letter was short and pointed: "the sad part is, there's a section of America who is cheering and celebrating right now, and that makes me sick to my stomach. We GOTTA get together y'all."

She later added, "btw stop saying we are not surprised. that's a damn shame in itself. I continue to be surprised at how little Black lives matter. And I will continue that. stop giving up on Black life."

And she concluded with "Black people. I love you. I love us. Our lives matter."

Patrice Cullors, Garza's friend, then connected those three words to a hashtag—#BlackLivesMatter—and another friend, Opal Tometi, built a social media platform that used the hashtag to connect likeminded activists to a new Black civil rights movement.

Demonstrating in Los Angeles following the acquittal of George Zimmerman.

The Black Lives Matter (BLM) movement came to national prominence after the police killing of Michael Brown in Ferguson, Missouri, on August 9, 2014. According to Garza, activists in Ferguson encouraged her and her friends to create a national organization with local chapters across the country. As more police shootings and murders of Black youths occurred in the following months—Ezell Ford, Akai Gurley, Tamir Rice, and Jerame Reid were among those killed—the movement spread and chapters formed across the nation. BLM now has chapters in every major region of the United States, and the overall movement has led or participated in thousands of protest marches, rallies, sit-ins, and die-ins: demonstrations where protesters lie motionless and silent on the ground pretending to be dead.

Thousands of students continue to help keep the movement alive and active. Their ongoing contributions make BLM one of the most important protest organizations in the United States and around the world. O

159

CHAPTER TEN

Running for Water

2016
*Anna Lee writes a letter to the
US Army Corps of Engineers*

2010   2015   2020

"**M**y name is Anna Lee Rain Yellowhammer. I'm 13 years old and I am an enrolled member of the Standing Rock Sioux Tribe. I lived all my life in Fort Yates, North Dakota."

Anna Lee had never written to the government before, but now she was sending a letter to the US Army Corps of Engineers.

"I am writing this letter to stop the Dakota Access Pipeline," she explained.

Anna Lee was a student at Standing Rock Middle School, and she had recently learned that a company named Energy Transfer was planning to build a 1,200-mile-long pipeline that would transport about 570,000 barrels of oil every day from North Dakota to Illinois. Project designs showed that the pipeline would run close to the Standing Rock Sioux Reservation in North Dakota, where she and her family lived. It would run under a dammed section of the Missouri River—the tribe's main source of water.

Like other Oceti Sakowin (the traditional term for the Sioux), Anna Lee believed that the pipeline could be dangerous to her home and community.

"If the pipeline breaks the oil will spill on the ground and into the water," she wrote in her letter. "Grass, crops, trees and animals will not be able to grow and live because of the oil. People will not be able to drink from the river or use the water. The time and the cost to clean up oil spills will take years and probably millions of dollars."

Anna Lee also stressed the importance of water by describing it as "the first medicine," essential for survival. *"Mní Wičóni"* she wrote in her native language. "Water is life."

She concluded her letter, dated April 9, 2016, with a bold invitation: "Say no to the Dakota Access Pipeline. Please sign our petition."

Anna Lee's grandmother had convinced her that a petition would be valuable in her fight against the Dakota Access Pipeline (DAPL). The right to petition our government is guaranteed in the First Amendment to the US Constitution. A petition is usually a short, written demand—for example, "Stop the construction of the Dakota Access Pipeline."

The makers of petitions usually try to get as many signatures as possible. More signatures prove that more citizens—and more voters—have noticed and care about an issue. The more signatures there are, the greater the chance that elected government officials will pay attention and make the requested change.

> ## The right to petition our government is guaranteed in the First Amendment to the US Constitution.

The federal government owned the land next to the reservation and under the Missouri River. Anna Lee addressed her "No DAPL" petition to the Army Corps of Engineers because they had the power to deny Energy Transfer's use of this federal land.

Along with thirty other Standing Rock kids, Anna Lee posted the petition on Change.org, an online platform where people can post, view, sign, and share petitions calling for positive social change.

A young woman named Bobbi Jean Three Legs helped Anna Lee spread the word about her petition. Three Legs and a handful of other young people lived night and day at Sacred Stone Camp, which they had pitched close to the planned route for the pipeline. There, they devoted themselves to spiritual activities that honored water and their ancestors. The small camp was their quiet way of opposing the pipeline and protecting their water.

Three Legs also founded an activist group called Rezpect Our Water. (*Rez* is the word that Native American kids often use to refer to their reservation.) Under her leadership, Rezpect created and posted videos that featured Standing Rock kids, including Anna Lee, asking viewers to sign the petition.

Rezpect's first video begins with a young girl singing in her Native language while beautiful pictures of the Standing Rock reservation and the Missouri River appear on screen. At the end, Tokata Iron Eyes, a twelve-year-old member of the Standing Rock Sioux Tribe, looks straight into the camera and confidently says, "Respect our water. Respect our land. And respect our people. Join us and sign our petition."

Tokata, Anna Lee, and their friends discovered that Energy Transfer had originally planned for the pipeline to run near Bismarck, North Dakota, but powerful white community leaders fought against it, claiming that an oil spill would ruin their drinking water. They persuaded Energy Transfer to change the route, moving the pipeline away from Bismarck and right next to Standing Rock. Like Anna Lee, Tokata found that news humiliating, and in the second video, she says, "It's like they [Energy Transfer] don't care as much about us."

While the videos went viral, Three Legs also used analog methods to share news about the petition—including a relay run. Throughout their history, Native Americans have used runners to deliver urgent messages. They have also employed relay runs, or "crow hops," when the distance that needs to be covered is too far for one runner to

Twelve-year-old Alice Brown Otter was one of the youngest runners to make the trip to the nation's capital.

do alone. The run is broken into sections, some runners can rest while others take their place.

In early April, Three Legs and two other members of Sacred Stone Camp, Joseph White Eyes and Jasilyn Charger, ran an eleven-mile relay around the Standing Rock reservation. Along the way, they talked to everyone they could about the pipeline and the plan to protect their water.

Encouraged by the support they received for this run, they planned a bigger one, a 564-mile relay that would end at the regional headquarters of the Army Corp of Engineers, in Omaha, Nebraska. Run for Your Life included about a dozen kids from all the different

Alice Brown Otter, left, and Anna Lee Rain Yellowhammer, right, hold the Standing Rock flag at a rally in Union Square in New York City. Bobbi Jean Three Legs is second from right.

bands, or parts, of the Oceti Sakowin, as well as some non-Native youth.

As the runners took off on April 24, Charger carried a wapaha, a wooden stick decorated with feathers, a sacred symbol representing all of their ancestors. The group believed that their deceased elders were with them in spirit, offering strength and courage for the journey ahead.

Each day, the group started their run at approximately 8:00 a.m. and covered between forty and eighty miles before stopping at around 8:00 p.m. Chaperones followed them in cars and vans and made sure they

Standing Rock activists often described themselves as "water protectors" rather than "protesters."

drank and ate healthily. The young activists ran from reservation to reservation, from small towns to big towns, often stopping to talk with local residents about Native American traditions, the importance of water, and the dangers of the pipeline. They invited local people of all ages to run along. At night, they slept anywhere that was offered to them, including private homes, churches, and community centers.

On May 3, eight days after starting, the runners arrived in Omaha for their scheduled appointment with Colonel John Henderson. Ten runners had made the entire trip, and about 160 had participated. Henderson

Ten runners had made the entire trip, and about 160 had participated.

failed to show up for the meeting, and the group was left to deliver their letter and petition to a Corps staff member on the steps of the office building.

"In North Dakota alone there have been three hundred oil spills in the last two years," the letter stated. "It is therefore not a matter of if the pipeline will break, but when, and how large the spill will be when it does." The runners demanded that the Corps conduct a full analysis of the environmental impact of the pipeline before making a final decision.

In the weeks that followed, Standing Rock youth focused on the need to attract national attention and support for their protest. In early June, Anna Lee helped this effort by writing an article calling for more signatures for the petition.

On July 7, Rezpect Our Water posted a dramatic announcement: Standing Rock youth would run from Sacred Stone Camp to Washington, DC. It would be a two-thousand-mile relay. One of the main purposes was to deliver Anna Lee's petition—which now had about 140,000 signatures—to the White House.

"We are now taking our message all the way to Washington, to the Corps' headquarters there and to

President Obama," Three Legs later explained. "To tell them to put an end to this act of aggression against our people, our land, our water, and our future."

Alice Brown Otter, a sixth grader at Standing Rock Middle School, asked her parents if she could join the run. She had been looking for a way to contribute to the movement, and this seemed like the perfect opportunity. At first, her parents were not enthusiastic. Alice, after all, was only twelve years old.

"If I don't do it, then who will?" she asked, trying to win their approval.

Assured that there would be adult chaperones, the Brown Otters agreed.

On July 16, about forty runners—named the Oceti Sakowin Youth and Allies—left Sacred Stone Camp. Anna Lee and Alice were part of the group.

There was excitement in the air, but the run was far from easy. The weather was hot and humid, and thunderstorms struck hard and fast. Runners got cramps and side stitches and sore feet.

"We're sacrificing our bodies to do this for humanity, for the people, for *Unci Maka*, Mother Earth," Three Legs explained.

The group tried to have at least three runners on the road, while the rest traveled in six support vehicles, drinking water and eating so that they would be prepared for their next turn. The goal was to cover between thirty and seventy miles a day, sometimes more.

As they ran from town to town, the runners carried three *wapaha* and chanted as a way to keep focus, share their message, and stay strong.

We run!
  We run!
For our people!
  For our people!
We run!
  We run!
For our nation!
  For our nation!
We run!
  We run!
For water!
  For water!
We run!
  We run!
For life!
  For life!

At the end of most days, the runners visited with local groups, giving talks about the need to protect Standing Rock's water. They also listened as local residents shared news about their own fights against the pipeline. In Iowa, a group of grandmothers recounted how they had been arrested during their protest.

The runners often felt a lot of support along their route. In some towns, residents ran with them. Some gave them Popsicles to cool them down. Some clapped and cheered. But other times people called them names, laughed at them, and said they would never make it to DC or stop the pipeline.

"It brought some of the runners down," Alice later reported. "We got really sad, but we kept going in prayer."

The runners slept overnight in homes, church basements, community centers, and hotels, and when nothing else was offered, they camped in tents. Sitting under the stars, they sang songs and shared stories, and discussed the run and their feelings about the protest.

On July 26, the runners were disappointed once again when they learned that the Army Corps of Engineers had given its approval for the construction of the pipeline. Some of them sobbed, while others turned to prayer.

But they would not go down in defeat.

As runner Joseph White Eyes remembered it, "All of a sudden we just stopped crying, got up and looked at each other and agreed we needed to keep going. And we jumped on the road."

They continued to tell their story to anyone who would listen. In Ohio, Alice spoke to a local reporter. "If the pipeline goes through, it could break our sacred sites," she explained, referring to places where her ancestors were buried. She added that the pipeline could hurt "our very important animals, our land, our plants and our people."

Alice also stressed that the Standing Rock youth would succeed in their mission. Like many of the other runners, she believed that long ago her ancestors had foretold that a great black snake would harm Mother Earth, and that her generation (known as the Seventh Generation) would rise up, reunite scattered tribes, defeat the snake, and save *Unci Maka*. To Alice and her friends, DAPL was the black snake.

As Alice and the runners placed their trust in their ancestors, they also had great confidence in President Barack Obama.

In 2014, the president and First Lady Michelle Obama had traveled to Standing Rock and talked with young people about their lives on the reservation. Runner Tariq Brownotter had the privilege of being in a small meeting with the president during his historic visit.

"It was an emotional meeting for all involved," she recalled. "We told him stories about our struggles on the reservation, and he cried with us when one of my friends talked about having to leave college in order to come home and care for his siblings after his mother became addicted to meth" (crystal methamphetamine, a dangerous and highly addictive illegal drug).

"Growing up on a Native American reservation, it was easy to feel like the rest of the country didn't care

Runners and allies protesting at the Army Corps of Engineers headquarters in Washington, DC.

about us," Tariq explained. "The Standing Rock reservation has very few resources for young people, and those that do exist are constantly shutting down for lack of funding. We have no teen center and few jobs or educational opportunities. Our people are dying of drug abuse and alcoholism. I've lost too many loved ones to suicide."

Tariq and her friends shared all this with the president and first lady.

"In response," she said, "the president told us about how he and Michelle had once felt like they were on the outside looking in, but by persistently raising their voices, they had been able to affect positive change for their communities and, ultimately, for the entire country. That day I knew I wanted to become a warrior for my people."

Inspired by the president, Tariq was running to the White House, trusting that President Obama would publicly show his support for their fight against the pipeline. She and her friends believed that he could—and would—help them.

When the runners were fifty miles from Washington, DC, they learned that the president would not meet with them. The news felt like a punch to the gut.

Still, they would not stop running.

But they did change course. Twenty-two days after leaving Sacred Stone Camp, the runners entered Washington, DC, and headed to the Corps of Engineers offices.

Outside the building, they chanted, "Can't drink oil! Keep it in the soil!"

They held the wapaha high. Some wrapped themselves in the light blue flag of the Standing Rock Sioux Tribe. Others played drums.

"We run!" they shouted. "For water!"

Passersby joined in, and the growing protest continued for hours.

"We knew that they [the Corps staff] were watching us," Alice recalled. "And we wouldn't stop."

Then, a surprise came. The major general of the Corps, as well as other leaders, said he would meet with the runners and hear their concerns.

The runners had had so many disappointments on their journey that the news was virtually unbelievable.

They happily walked across the street for a meeting inside the National Building Museum.

"All the youths got a minute to talk," Alice said.

They told the Major General and Corps staff members about reservation life, the significance of water, their fears about the pipeline, and their hopes and dreams for a healthy life. White Eyes spoke passionately about Native American history—about all the treaties that the US government had broken, about the decades of pain and suffering that followed, and about the need for the government to make things right for his people. His talk, coupled with all the other comments, had a powerful effect.

"We just changed a lot of minds," Alice said. "They started crying, and it opened a lot of their hearts, and they listened to us, and it felt like we mattered again."

The group then did what they had run all those miles to do—they delivered their petition, which now had more than 160,000 signatures, to the people who had the power to stop the pipeline.

Meanwhile, the race had helped to raise so much awareness that Sacred Stone Camp was soon too crowded to hold everyone who wanted to be there. A newer camp across the river also grew by leaps and bounds. Hundreds and then thousands of activists—they called themselves "water protectors"—came to live at the camps and hold peaceful demonstrations against the DAPL.

Some young people at the camps, including those who had not run to DC, created the International

Oceta Sakowin youth and allies take a symbolic run in New York City after completing the relay to Washington, DC.

Indigenous Youth Council (IIYC). Their role was not only to plan and lead protests but also to help keep demonstrators calm when they became too heated or prone to violence.

Back in Washington, Obama still did not publicly oppose the pipeline. In early September, Alice expressed her disappointment to a group of Standing Rock leaders.

"We know he's listening to us, but he isn't speaking out and helping us," she said. "He said that he'd do anything for us, but where is he now?"

On September 9, the president finally issued an executive order that temporarily blocked the construction of DAPL on federal lands. He also called for additional input from the tribe.

It was a victory, but only a temporary one. The protesters knew that Energy Transfer would fight the order

Back in Washington, Obama still did not publicly oppose the pipeline.

in court while continuing to build the pipeline in other places. So the demonstrations continued.

The protests at the pipeline construction area next to the camps sometimes grew tense and dangerous. Members of the IIYC were injured when a private security team hired by the company sicced dogs on them. Police officers, also guarding the DAPL, shot them with rubber bullets, small sandbags, and pepper spray.

"I'm willing to set my life on the line to protect this water, to protect . . . Mother Earth," said Terrell Iron Shell, an IIYC leader.

On December 4, the Department of the Army announced that it would not grant permission for the Dakota Access Pipeline to run under the tribe's main water source. "The best way to complete that work responsibly . . . is to explore alternate routes for the pipeline crossing," said Jo-Ellen Darcy, a leader in the department.

The Standing Rock kids whooped and hollered, cried and cheered, hugged and held one another. Tokata Iron Eyes, now thirteen, felt overwhelmed. It had been such a long, painful journey since she'd appeared in the first

Police officers, also guarding the DAPL, shot them with rubber bullets, small sandbags, and pepper spray.

Rezpect Our Water video. "I feel like I got my future back," she said.

And then her tears started to flow.

The joy did not last long. On January 24, 2017, just days after he assumed office, President Donald Trump signed an executive order allowing the construction of the DAPL to proceed on federal property. The Standing Rock movement was furious. Protesters flooded the streets of Washington, DC, and the tribe filed a lawsuit in federal court.

On July 6, 2020, a judge ruled that the pipeline must shut down and be emptied of oil by August 5, 2020, and that the government must conduct and complete a review of the environmental effects of the pipeline. Water protectors at Standing Rock breathed a deep sigh of relief, knowing that environmental reviews could take years to complete.

Although the future of DAPL remained uncertain, the Oceti Sakowin youth could drink clean water and safely swim and play and fish in the river. They could enjoy what they had proclaimed to the rest of America: "*Mní Wičóni* —Water is life." O

CHAPTER ELEVEN

The Women's March

2017
*More than four million people
participate in the march*

2010   2015   2020

Protest signs bobbed up and down as the massive crowd strode toward the Washington Monument during the 2017 Women's March. One of the signs, held by a girl, summed up a lot of the strong statements made that day: FEMINISM IS THE RADICAL NOTION THAT WOMEN ARE EQUAL.

The feminist marchers also shouted many chants and replies. Some of the best ones mentioned girls.

Who's the boss of girls?
Girls the boss of girls!

Girls rule!
Girls rule!

Girls just want
Fundamental human rights!

On January 21, 2017, the first full day of Donald Trump's presidency, more than four million people—including thousands of kids—participated in the Women's March on Washington and its "sister marches" across the nation and the world. Scholars Erica Chenoweth and Jeremy Pressman describe the event as "likely the largest single-day demonstration in recorded US history."

A positive message at the Women's March in New York City.

The main march took place at the nation's capital, but marches in Los Angeles, Oakland, San Francisco, New York City, Chicago, Denver, Seattle, and Boston each attracted more than one hundred thousand protesters.

Some of the marches took place under very difficult circumstances. Chenoweth and Pressman note that five people marched in a cancer ward in Los Angeles; two thousand marched in below-zero temperatures in Fairbanks, Alaska; and forty marched in a wind chill of forty below zero in Unalakleet, Alaska.

Across America, protesters marched partly because the new president had demeaned women before and during his campaign.

Across America, protesters marched partly because the new president had demeaned women before and during his campaign. Before his campaign, Trump had bragged about grabbing women and touching them without their consent, which is a crime. During his campaign, he had also made inappropriate comments about his Republican opponent Carly Fiorina. "Look at that face! Would anyone vote for that? Can you imagine that, the face of our next president?" He also made vulgar comments about news anchor Megyn Kelly after she pointed out that Trump had referred to some women as "fat pigs, dogs, slobs, and disgusting animals."

Many of the protesters at the women's march were also frustrated because Democratic candidate Hillary Rodham Clinton had not won the presidency. They were outraged that a man with no direct qualifications for the presidency had won the election over a woman who was extremely well qualified for the Oval Office.

After the election, millions of voters worried that women's rights were in danger. During the campaign

Signs were everywhere in the massive crowd of more than half a million people.

Trump had promised to appoint federal judges who would seek to overturn a legal right to abortion, and once he was inaugurated, he would have the chance to do just that.

One of these concerned women was Teresa Shook of Hawaii. Right after the election, she posted on Facebook that the country needed a pro-women march. She then created a Facebook group and extended invitations. By the next morning, about ten thousand people had committed to attending the march. With the numbers continuing to swell, veteran activists formed a national committee and organized the event.

Because this march had a wide focus, covering many issues instead of one or two specific ones, the organizers wrote this about its mission: "We believe that Women's Rights are Human Rights and Human Rights are Women's Rights. We must create a society in which women—including Black women, Native women, poor women, immigrant women, disabled women, Muslim women, lesbian, queer, and trans women—are free and able to care for and nurture their families, however they are formed, in safe and healthy environments."

This statement expanded the basic purpose of the march to call for protecting women's rights beyond those encroached upon by sexism. The march called for workers' rights, civil rights, disability rights, immigrant rights, and LGBTQ+ rights.

The march officially began at 10:00 a.m. with a rally near the US Capitol. Speakers for the day included activists, politicians, filmmakers, actors, and singers. Representing diverse backgrounds, they expressed their support for women's rights and representation.

Signs were everywhere in the massive crowd of more than half a million people. A girl in a pink coat held one made of cardboard that read, I CAN BE PRESIDENT. Hundreds of other girls also held signs. Some of their messages read, GIRL POWER; KIDS CARE; I AM POWERFUL AND VALUABLE; I CHOOSE KINDNESS; EQUALITY + INCLUSION = LIBERTY.

One girl held a sign reading, I VOTE IN EIGHT YEARS. She wore a pink beanie with cat ears. The women who designed this popular hat—thousands wore it to the march—created it as a symbol of "support and solidarity for women's rights and political resistance."

Speaking for transgender rights, activist Janet Mock delivered one of the more powerful speeches of the day: "My sisters and siblings are being beaten, brutalized, neglected and invisibilized, extinguished, and exiled. My sisters and siblings have been pushed out of hostile homes and intolerant schools. My sisters and siblings have been forced into detention facilities and prisons and deeper into poverty. And I hold these harsh

185

truths close. They enrage me and fuel me, but I cannot survive on righteous anger alone. Today, by being here, it is my commitment to getting us free that keeps me marching."

Another speaker was six-year-old Sofía Cruz, the daughter of undocumented immigrants from Mexico. She had been invited to speak partly because she was already well known as an activist.

With help from an immigrant-rights group in September 2015, Sofía had traveled to the nation's capital from her home in Los Angeles. She wanted to meet Pope Francis and ask him to help her father and other undocumented immigrants, people who had entered the United States illegally.

As the Pope's car approached the place where the Cruz family was standing, Sofía's father helped her over the barricade that separated the crowd from the procession. Wearing a traditional red Mexican dress, Sofía took a step toward the Pope's car, but a security guard blocked her.

Then Pope Francis spotted her and motioned for her to come to him. The crowd cheered as the security guard lifted Sofía up and carried her to the Pope.

Pope Francis gave her a kiss on the cheek, and she gave him a big hug before handing him a letter she had written. Part of the letter read, "Pope Francis, I want to tell you that my heart is sad . . . I would like to ask you to speak to the president and the Congress in legalizing my parents, because every day I am scared that one day they will take them away from me."

Double the Girl Power at the Women's March in Washington, DC.

As videos of her meeting with the Pope went viral, people from across the world became aware of Sofía and her fear that the government would take her parents. She helped people understand the struggles of undocumented immigrants in the United States. She also encouraged the Pope to speak up on behalf of immigrants.

Eight months later, the White House invited Sofía to join them for Cinco de Mayo, the yearly celebration of Mexico's independence, history, and culture. Her parents had been hoping to go with her, but they were not allowed inside. They were still undocumented immigrants, so they did not have the paperwork required to enter the president's home.

Sofía Cruz and her family on the main stage of the Women's March in Washington, DC.

"We are here together making a chain of love to protect our families."

Outside the White House, Cruz's father spoke about Sofía. "Her mind is very powerful, and her imagination is amazing," he said. "She fights for her dreams."

Another eight months after visiting the White House, Sofía was once again back in Washington, DC. Her reputation as an advocate for immigrants had earned her an invitation from the organizers of the Women's March on Washington.

Sofía beamed as she stood front and center on the march's main stage.

"Hi, everybody!" she said.

The crowd cheered.

Standing behind her were her proud parents and her little sister. All of them were wearing traditional Mexican clothing. Sofía, also known as Sophie, was sporting a bright red coat.

"My name is Sophie Cruz," she said. "We are here together making a chain of love to protect our families. Let us fight with love, faith, and courage so that our families will not be destroyed."

Then she added, "I also want to tell the children not to be afraid, because we are not alone. There are still many people that have their hearts filled with love and

Many marchers across the country wore pink beanies with cat ears.

tenderness to snuggle in this path of life. Let's keep together and fight for the rights. God is with us!"

Sofía then brought a tear to her mother's eye as she delivered the same comments in Spanish. The crowd loved listening to her, and they joined her as she led them in a chant of *"¡Si, se puede! ¡Si, se puede! ¡Si, se puede!"* Yes, we can!

"Thank you," Sofía concluded. *"¡Gracias!"*

As she turned to leave the stage, the crowd cheered, "Sophie! Sophie! Sophie!"

As the rally ended, the march began. Because the crowd was so thick, the organizers could not lead the

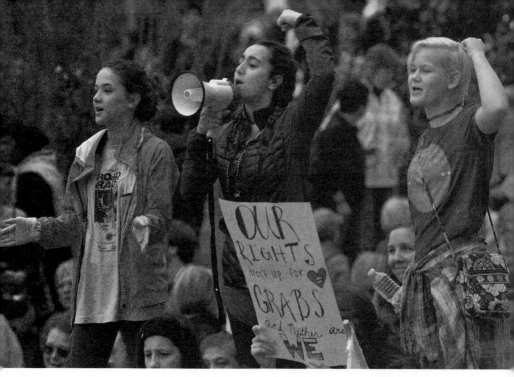

Cheering with a megaphone at the Women's March in Charlotte, North Carolina.

way as they had planned; instead, masses of people made their way to the Washington Monument.

One of the marchers was eight-year-old Hazel Merritt from Tacoma Park, Maryland. When asked by a reporter, Merritt said she was marching "because I am a girl, and I like having women's rights."

After the historic march, many of the protesters went back to their communities and organized voters in support of politicians who were pro-women's rights. They did not win any major legislative victories in Congress, but they continued to pressure politicians by lobbying, filing lawsuits, and holding marches in Washington every January. ○

The March for Our Lives

2018

*The shooter kills fourteen students
and three staff members*

2010   2015   2020

On Valentine's Day 2018, a nineteen-year-old walked into the freshman building at Marjory Stoneman Douglas High School (SD) in Parkland, Florida. He carried a bulky black bag that held an AR-15 rifle and more than three hundred rounds of ammunition. The young man suffered from mental illness, he had been expelled from the school, and he was about to commit a horrendous crime.

On the first floor of the building, he stood at the doors of two classrooms and fired into each. In an empty second-floor hallway, he fired into two more classrooms, injuring no one. He then moved to the third floor, where students and teachers, because they had not heard the shots, had poured into the hallway, thinking that the blaring alarms signaled a fire drill. The gunman fired into the chaotic crowd.

By this point, about six minutes after entering the school, the shooter had killed fourteen students and three staff members, and he had injured another fifteen. No law enforcement officer had yet entered the building.

The killer then ditched his rifle, exited the building, and blended into the crowd of fleeing students. A little more than an hour later, a police officer arrested him, finally ending one of the deadliest school shootings in US history.

Student David Hogg, director of SD's student news, used his phone to report on the shooting while the school was still in lockdown. "At around 2:30, we heard a gunshot in my AP environmental science class, and we initially thought it was a drill," he explained in the video. "And then we heard . . . more gunshots, and that was when we realized this was not a drill. This was life or death."

Hogg also interviewed students who were with him in the darkened room. One of them described an intense transformation she was undergoing in that traumatic moment: "I personally have rallied for gun rights, and this has definitely changed my viewpoint," she explained. "We need more gun control in our country."

Hogg then turned the camera back on himself and said: "I call on the legislators of this country to take action and stop this from happening. Forget the NRA. Forget all the political backing. Thousands of people have died from gun violence, and it's time to take a stand."

That evening, junior class president Jaclyn Corin grew frustrated as she watched news about the shooting and saw that her fellow students were posting prayers on social media with the hashtag #DouglasStrong. Corin decided to do more than pray, and she used her

Instagram and Facebook pages to protest. She posted a picture with the words *Make It Stop* above an image of a semiautomatic rifle. Her message below read: "Contact your state and local representatives, as we must have stricter gun laws immediately. We need to work together to bring change to this country so that something like this never happens again."

On the night of February 15, thousands of people gathered for a candlelight vigil. Student body president Julia Cordover solemnly spoke the names of the seventeen victims. Religious leaders led prayers, and other adults called for mental health reform and gun control laws. After US Representative Deborah Wasserman Schultz delivered a speech about holding elected officials accountable for school shootings, many in the crowd shouted: "No more guns! No more guns! No more guns!"

As the vigil ended, theater student Cameron Kasky, who had been posting on social media virtually nonstop since the shooting, asked a few friends to head back to his house. He wanted to jumpstart a movement focused on ending school shootings. "Stay alert," he posted. "#NeverAgain." Before long, Stoneman Douglas students active on social media, including Sarah Chadwick, Sofie Whitney, and John Barnitt, set up a collective Twitter account they named @NeverAgainMSD.

On the morning of February 16, Jaclyn Corin contacted a state senator and explained that she was planning to lead a group of SD students on a trip to the state capitol in Tallahassee, where they would urge politicians to adopt stricter gun control laws. Corin invited her classmates to join her, and the response was so overwhelming that she had to cap the trip at one hundred students.

Throughout the day, Corin and other SD student leaders gave one interview after another, appearing on national and international media outlets. They knew that if they did not keep the story alive, the media's attention would soon move on. In his interviews, David Hogg criticized President Donald Trump and legislators for not calling for new gun control laws. "He didn't even mention guns," Hogg said, referring to a statement the president had made about the shooting. "These are children's lives being taken and nothing is being done. Now is the time for action. If our legislators don't take action, how can we ever feel safe?" As he spoke, other activists held signs, reading, MAKE SCHOOL SAFE and KIDS DON'T NEED GUNS.

That night, a group of students—Kasky, Sofie Whitney, Alex Wind, Alphonso Calderon, Ryan Deitsch, Brendan and Daniel Duff, and SD alum Kaylyn Pipitone—went out to a Chinese restaurant and planned the next steps in their budding movement. During a long brainstorming session, the group settled on a bold idea: a national march on Washington.

During a long brainstorming session, the group settled on a bold idea: a national march on Washington.

Back home, Kasky invited Corin to join them in organizing the march. She arrived twenty minutes later, joining the group of energized teens sprawled out across Kasky's living room.

On Saturday, February 17, the Broward County School Board staged a large rally at the federal courthouse. The crowd cheered as a variety of speakers called for stricter gun control laws. The highlight of the day came when SD senior Emma González delivered a speech criticizing politicians for being soft on gun control. Standing in front of a brown podium with a US flag attached to it, González clutched her speech in her left hand. She wiped her eyes every now and then as she spoke with passion and clarity.

> We certainly do not understand why it should be harder to make plans with friends on weekends than to buy an automatic or semi-automatic weapon. In Florida,

to buy a gun, you do not need a permit, you do not need a gun license, and once you buy it, you do not need to register it. You do not need a permit to carry a concealed rifle or shotgun. You can buy as many guns as you want at one time . . .

The people in the government are lying to us. And us kids seem to be the only ones who notice and are prepared to call B.S. . . . Politicians who sit in the gilded House and Senate seats funded by the NRA, telling us nothing could have been done to prevent this—we call B.S.! They say tougher gun laws do not decrease gun violence—we call B.S.! They say a good guy with a gun stops a bad guy with a gun—we call B.S.! They say guns are just tools like knives and are as dangerous as cars—we call B.S.! They say no laws could have prevented the hundreds of senseless tragedies that have occurred—we call B.S.! That us kids don't know what we're talking about, that we're too young to understand how the government works—we call B.S.!

At the end of González's speech, the crowd expressed its full-throated anger at the politicians who dismissed the need for stricter gun control measures. "Throw them out!" the students yelled. "Throw them out!"

A few hours later, Kasky invited González to join the core students working on the march. Hogg joined, too. Kasky's living room now held sleeping bags, pillows, and lots of snacks. The scene looked like a slumber party, but the work that the kids were doing was serious.

Leaders of the March for Our Lives celebrating the conclusion of the main rally in Washington, DC.

The call for new legislation continued the following day when five members of the core leadership—Kasky, González, Hogg, Corin, and Wind—appeared on national television networks, including ABC, CBS, and CNN, to announce the march.

"People are saying that it's not time to talk about gun control, and we can respect that," Kasky told ABC. "Here's a time: March 24th. In every single city, we are going to be marching together as students begging for our lives."

González added that the students had set up a website so that interested people could learn about plans for the march. "Students all over the country are going to be joining us," she said. "We are going to shoulder this heavy burden, and we are going to do it well." The website for the march read:

"We are going to shoulder this heavy burden, and we are going to do it well."

Not one more. We cannot allow one more child to be shot at school. We cannot allow one more teacher to make a choice to jump in front of a firing assault rifle to save the lives of students. We cannot allow one more family to wait for a call or text that never comes. Our schools are unsafe. Our children and teachers are dying. We must make it our top priority to save these lives.

. . . On March 24, the kids and families of March for Our Lives will take to the streets of Washington, DC to demand that their lives and safety become a priority . . .

Stand with us on March 24. Refuse to allow one more needless death. March for our lives!

In addition to announcing the March for Our Lives, the students also said that they would continue to call out and criticize politicians, Democratic and Republican, who accepted money from the National Rifle Association rather than passing sensible gun control legislation. Among those politicians was Trump, who had taken to Twitter to blame Democrats for failing to pass gun control laws during the Obama presidency.

When asked about Trump's comment, Hogg said, "President Trump, you control the House of

Representatives, you control the Senate, and you control the executive. You haven't taken a single bill for mental health care or gun control and passed it. And that's pathetic . . . Are you kidding me? Do you think now is the time to focus on the past and not the future to prevent the deaths of thousands of other children?"

Donations began to pour in, and the students set up a crowdfunding campaign that quickly raised millions of dollars for the march. A local businessperson donated an empty office to serve as the march headquarters, and attorneys offered free legal services.

The students also turned to an experienced television producer, Deena Katz, to help them plan the event. She applied for the permit for the march in Washington within a week of its announcement.

As planning for the march took off, Jaclyn Corin finalized the details for the lobbying trip to the state capital. On Tuesday afternoon, February 20, just six days after the shooting, one hundred Stoneman Douglas students, carrying pillows and sleeping bags, left on three coach buses for the four-hundred-mile ride to Tallahassee.

On the way there, the students learned that the Florida House of Representatives had just rejected a motion to consider a bill banning assault rifles. It wasn't an actual bill that they had rejected: it was the idea of even debating or drafting such a bill. "That's infuriating," said junior Anthony Lopez. "They're acting inhuman."

Despite the Florida Legislature's decision, the students had the nation's attention and sympathy—especially from other kids. A large group of Tallahassee students had gathered to welcome the Stoneman Douglas protesters as the three buses pulled into the parking lot. It was the first time that Corin had seen such strong in-person support from a community outside Parkland, and she felt gratified and inspired.

The SD students then headed to the local civic center, where the Red Cross had set up cots for their overnight stay. Too excited to sleep, many of them chatted into the early morning hours.

On the morning of February 21, the students divided into groups of ten or so and spent the day urging Democratic and Republican lawmakers to ban AR-15s and pass new restrictions on other guns. Some of the meetings upset the students.

When Senator Debbie Mayfield spoke about the possibility of raising the minimum age to purchase

Too excited to sleep, many of them chatted into the early morning hours.

guns, student Daniel Bishop replied that the change would not prevent mass shootings. Mayfield dismissed the criticism, saying, "We can't stop the crazies" (people with psychological disabilities). Hearing those words, student Amanda De La Cruz and others felt deflated. "I want the ban on semiautomatic weapons," she said. "I don't care about the crazies."

After their meetings, the students headed to the House floor, where Richard Corcoran, the Speaker of the House, took questions. Sixteen-year-old Alondra Gittelson asked, "I just want to know why such a destructive gun is accessible to the public—why that gun, the AR-15, that did so much damage, how is an individual in society able to acquire such a gun?"

Corcoran explained that he was opposed to banning guns like the one used at Stoneman Douglas. "I think that if you look, it's widely used in multiple different hunting scenarios," he said. "I know people who go out and they'll do boar hunts and they'll use them."

While the students were not opposing the rights of hunters, they were shocked that the desire to permit boar hunting with AR-15s outweighed the necessity of preventing human slaughter.

Hundreds of other students also arrived that afternoon to protest. Flooding the hallways and offices of the capitol, they carried signs and petitions calling for gun reform. When they reached the office of Governor Rick Scott, they filled the reception area and shouted, "Shame! Shame! Shame!"

The last meeting that the SD students had scheduled for the day was with the governor. He refused to commit to an assault weapons ban but appeared to back mental health reforms.

By the end of the meeting, the students were spent. It had been a long day, and many legislators had been unwilling to advocate for the laws they requested. As they headed back home, Corin realized that the fight would be far from easy.

That night, members of the Stoneman Douglas community appeared at an internationally televised town hall hosted by CNN. It proved to be another chance for SD students to confront politicians, this time US senators and a US representative, about their stance on the National Rifle Association and gun control.

Dressed in a dark purple shirt with a black tie, Cameron Kasky put the issue directly to Florida Senator Marco Rubio. "So, Senator Rubio, can you tell me right now that you will not accept a single donation from the NRA in the future?" Many in the audience applauded the question, and when Rubio did not answer it directly, the cheers turned to boos.

"In the name of seventeen people," Kasky replied, "you cannot ask the NRA to keep their money out of your campaign?" Rubio did not commit to refusing donations from the NRA, and the audience booed yet again.

Then student Chris Grady asked his question of the senator: "Would you agree that there is no place in our society for large-capacity magazines capable of firing . . . from fifteen to thirty rounds, if not more?"

In a reply that shocked many, the senator said that he was "reconsidering" his earlier position on permitting the purchase of large-capacity magazines. Banning large-capacity magazines, he said, would not prevent a gun assault, but "it may save lives in an attack."

This time, the audience cheered.

On Sunday, February 25, senior Ryan Deitsch and his brother Matt led a handful of students, including senior Delaney Tarr, on a quiet lobbying trip to Washington, DC. Bonding with the other students gave Tarr the first feeling of happiness she had experienced since the shooting.

The students met with about two hundred members of Congress during their two-day stay. The results were mixed. Sometimes the students felt as if the members of Congress listened to them, and other times they were lectured about the Second Amendment and the right to "bear arms."

The students were especially disappointed by their meeting with House Speaker Paul Ryan. They urged him to pass legislation that would ban AR-15s and high-capacity magazines, and support background checks for anyone who wanted to buy a gun. They also asked Ryan to schedule a gun-control debate and vote on gun-control bills. But Ryan would not commit. He focused instead on mental health policies.

However, the students had an inspiring meeting with Representative John Lewis of Georgia, who, during the 1960s civil rights movement, had served as chairman of the Student Nonviolent Coordinating Committee and led many student marches against racial discrimination. In their meeting with Lewis, some of the students cried as he drew connections between the historic civil rights movement and the March for Our Lives.

A little more than a week later, Governor Scott broke ranks with the National Rifle Association and signed legislation that raised the minimum age to purchase a gun from eighteen to twenty-one. The new law—named the Marjory Stoneman Douglas High School Public Safety Act—also created a waiting period of three days for prospective gun buyers; banned bump stocks, a device that makes it possible for guns to fire faster; permitted

Somber activists sharing their messages at the march in Washington, DC.

superintendents and sheriffs to arm school personnel; and provided funding for hiring safety officers, building safer buildings, and expanding mental health care to students.

SD students and their families attended the signing of the legislation, and Governor Scott told them, "You made your voices heard. You didn't let up and you fought until there was change. You helped change our state. You made a difference. You should be proud." Rebecca Schneid, the editor of the SD newspaper, said the bill was "not perfect" but that she supported what it did accomplish. "I never really expected them to get something done so fast," she said.

On March 14, tens of thousands of students from about 2,800 schools across the country participated in a walkout to mark the one-month anniversary of the SD shooting.

In Washington, DC, hundreds of students held a silent sit-in in front of the White House. They sat for seventeen minutes, one minute for each victim of the shooting. Breaking the silence at 10:17, they shouted, "We want change!" They then marched up Pennsylvania Avenue and gathered with other students to rally at the US Capitol. There, many of the activists chanted, "Hey hey, ho ho! Gun violence has got to go!"

One student sharing a megaphone sobbed as she told the crowd that she felt afraid at school every day since the SD shooting. "That is not okay," she said. "That is not okay."

At Columbine High School in Colorado, where one of the first mass school shootings had taken place nineteen years earlier, students walked to a nearby soccer field and released red, white, and blue balloons to memorialize the SD victims. Columbine student Leah Zundel said, "We should never go to school in fear of our lives. Enough is enough."

More than two thousand students at Stoneman Douglas walked out of their classes and headed to the campus football field. Cameron Kasky tweeted, "To the parents supporting their children walking out, thank you for raising this new generation of leaders. To the parents who didn't support their children who walked out anyway, thank you for raising this new generation of leaders."

The morning of March 24 was cold and sunny in Washington, DC. For some, it was also full of fear. "To be honest, I'm scared to march," SD student Carly Novell wrote online. "This is a march against gun violence, and I am scared there will be gun violence on the march. This is just my mindset living in this country right now, but this is why we need to march." Novell's fear was not irrational; SD student leaders had received hate mail and even death threats while planning the march.

But most of the student leaders were excited that morning. They had spent the night before practicing their speeches, encouraging one another, and sharing memories of all the work they had accomplished. Now, they were ready to make history.

They were not sure how many had descended on Washington for their march. Some worried that not many people would attend, but as they made their way to Pennsylvania Avenue, where the stage was located, they saw one city block after another crowded with activists. "It was a never-ending stream of people," said Sofie Whitney.

Hundreds of thousands of concerned students and their allies had come to DC for the March for Our Lives. The crowd near the stage was packed so tight that the SD students could see heat shimmering above the mass of bodies before them. The scene left student Dylan Baierlein breathless.

Chris Grady was "blown away" when he saw the stage. It featured large banners reading MARCH FOR OUR LIVES, jumbotrons for broadcasting speeches and performances, and a single podium adorned only with a paper sign that also read, MARCH FOR OUR LIVES. Positioned perfectly in the open background was the Capitol, surrounded by bright blue skies.

Together, the SD students marched toward an area designated for student organizers, shooting victims, and teachers and mentors from around the country. Just five weeks earlier, they had been hiding in dark rooms, too afraid to speak above a whisper, but now, in the bright of day, they were shouting, "Who are we? MSD!" The crowd cleared a path for them as they made their way to the stage.

Backstage, where speakers and celebrity performers mingled with one another, the feeling was electric. Cameron Kasky was the first speaker of the day. The massive crowd shouted their support as he began.

"To the leaders, skeptics, and cynics who told us to sit down and stay silent, wait your turn: Welcome to the revolution!" he began. "It is a powerful one because it is of, by, and for the young people of this country."

Kasky pumped up the crowd all the more when he offered a reply to critics who wondered whether March for Our Lives would change anything. "Look around," he said. "We are the change!"

The most powerful part of his speech came when he delivered an ultimatum to the country's lawmakers. "Politicians, either represent the people or get out!" he said. "The people demand a law banning the sale of assault weapons. The people demand we prohibit the sale of high-capacity magazines. The people demand

Hundreds of thousands of concerned students and their allies had come to DC for the March for Our Lives.

universal background checks. Stand for us or beware: the voters are coming!"

As Kasky left the stage, Delaney Tarr, the next SD student in line to speak, was acting cool, calm, and collected, even though she was "freaking out inside." To make matters worse, when she put her speech on the podium, the wind blew it halfway across the stage. After retrieving it and settling down, Tarr spoke with pure passion. "Today, we march, we fight, we *roar!*" she said. "We prepare our signs. We raise them high. We know what we want, we know how to get it, and we are not waiting any longer."

As a show of support, thousands of students raised their signs high—homemade signs, manufactured signs, signs on sticks, cardboard cutouts—all of them carrying similar messages: WHAT DO YOU LIKE MORE, GUNS OR KIDS?; ARMS ARE FOR HUGGING; PROTEST GUNS, NOT KIDS; AM I NEXT?; ONE CHILD IS WORTH MORE THAN ALL THE GUNS; HOW MANY MORE?; WE ARE HUMANS, NOT TARGETS; STOP THE NRA; GUNS ARE THE DEATH OF U.S.; and #ENOUGHISENOUGH.

Three friends stood side-by-side, each holding part of a longer message: MURDERED IN SCHOOL; AND STILL

Two peaceful fists at the march in Washington, DC.

NO GUN LAWS; HOW COME, CONGRESS? Three other friends did the same: PLEASE; DON'T; SHOOT.

SD students were not the only ones to speak. During the run-up to the march, they had formed alliances with students from all over the country and invited several to share their stories and represent their communities onstage.

Trevon Bosley, a high schooler whose brother had been shot and killed, used his time to talk about his peers from Chicago. "I'm here to speak for those youth who fear they may be shot while going to the gas station, the movies, the bus stop, to church, or even to and from school," he said. "I'm here to speak for those Chicago youth who feel their voices have been silenced for far too long."

Edna Chávez, a senior from Manual Arts High School in Los Angeles, quieted the crowd when she said that she learned how to duck from bullets before she learned how

"Politicians, either represent the people or get out!"

to read, and that it was normal for those in her neighborhood "to see flowers honoring the lives of Black and brown youth that have lost their lives to a bullet."

Chávez also spoke movingly of her brother, a victim of gun violence. "Ricardo was his name," she said. "Can you all say it with me?" Tears flowed down her cheeks as the crowd shouted his name again and again.

Jaclyn Corin shared some of her stage time with a very special guest: Yolanda Renee King, the granddaughter of Martin Luther King Jr. and Coretta Scott King. Just a few days earlier, after she had watched an inspiring video of Yolanda leading a chant, Corin reached out and invited her to come to the march. That hasty invitation led to one of the highlights of the march.

"I have a dream," the nine-year-old King said, echoing her grandfather, "that enough is enough, and that this world should be a gun-free world, period!" She then asked the crowd to repeat her words: "Spread the word! Have you heard? All across the nation! We! Are Going to Be! A Great Generation!" Infected by her hope, the crowd smiled and laughed and cheered.

The last speaker for the day was Emma González. Before heading onto the stage, she had been crying, touched by the emotions of the day, as well as by the raw memories of February 14. But when the time came, she strode to the podium with confidence and steeliness, determined to let the protesters know exactly why they were there.

"Six minutes and about twenty seconds," she began. "In a little over six minutes, seventeen of our friends were taken from us, fifteen more were injured, and everyone, absolutely everyone in the Douglas community was forever changed. Everyone who has been touched by the cold grip of violence understands."

What Emma understood—and what she wanted everyone else to acknowledge—was the depth of personal pain and suffering caused by the shooting. Never again, she said, would her friend Carmen complain to her about piano practice. Never again would each of the seventeen victims—and she named each of them—be able to enjoy the friendships that had sustained them. Never again.

And then Emma went silent.

Looking straight ahead, with tears running down her cheeks, she led the crowd in a long moment of silence.

Just silence.

When she brought that powerful moment to an end, she concluded, "Since the time I came out here, it has been six minutes and twenty seconds," she said. "The shooter has ceased shooting and will soon abandon his rifle, blend in with the students as they escape, and

Emma González during the silent part of her speech at the March for Our Lives in Washington, DC.

walk free for an hour before arrest. Fight for your lives before it's someone else's job."

The crowd erupted.

To end the day, singer Jennifer Hudson—whose mother and brother had been killed by gun violence—joined a DC choir onstage for a gospel-inspired version of Bob Dylan's song, "The Times They Are a-Changin'." In the middle of the song, Hudson added her own commentary. "We all came here for change," she said. "We're all here for a reason: change."

At that point, the stage manager turned to the Stoneman Douglas students, as well as other students nearby, and instructed them to join Hudson onstage. The students happily obliged and led the sea of people before them in a chant of "We want change!"

Beyond Washington, DC, students across the country were shaking up their own communities with public rallies, demanding stricter gun control laws and safer schools. Numbering more than 750, these rallies occurred in every state and every continent except for Antarctica. More than 150,000 marched in New York City alone.

There were counterprotests, too—about forty of them. In Salt Lake City, Utah, hundreds of people attended a gun rights rally. In Boston, where gun rights activists gathered at the State House, protester Paul Allen said: "We believe in the Second Amendment. You people will interpret it the way you want, and we'll interpret it for what it is—that law-abiding citizens who are true patriots have the right to bear arms."

But the 2,500 counterprotesters that day were overshadowed by the two million activists who attended March for Our Lives events across the globe. The student-led March for Our Lives was the largest-ever single-day protest for gun control. The Stoneman Douglas students had made history.

And they planned to continue making history.

At the March for Our Lives event in Parkland, Florida, SD sophomore Sari Kaufman urged the protesters to "turn this moment into a movement" that would drive NRA-supported politicians from office. Seventeen-year-old Casey Sherman made a similar point. "Those seventeen people did not die in vain. We will stop at nothing until we make real, lasting change."

By early summer, SD students were making good on their promise. They took a nationwide bus tour—Road to Change—to register voters and enlist support for their policy goals. These goals ranged from funding gun violence research to banning high-capacity magazines to disarming anyone with a record of domestic violence. Road to Change lasted two months, visited fifty cities, and registered about fifty thousand young voters.

At the end of the summer, the Pew Charitable Trusts credited the SD students and the March for Our Lives movement for creating "a year of unparalleled success for the gun control movement." That success included the passage of almost fifty new gun control laws in twenty-five states.

Since then, the March for Our Lives movement has continued. Hundreds of chapters have formed throughout the country. In each state, they fight for change on the local level and join one another in an ongoing national and international campaign for safe schools and a reduction in gun violence. O

CHAPTER THIRTEEN

School Strike 4 Climate

2019
*Battery Park is filled with
about 250,000 climate strikers*

2010   2015   2020

The Camp Fire began in the northern part of the state, in the Sierra Nevada foothills, during the early morning hours of November 8, 2018. Caused by a nearly one-hundred-year-old electrical transmission line, the fire spread quickly. At its peak, it burned at a rate of eighty football fields per minute. It took thousands of firefighters seventeen days to contain it.

The fire was able to move so fast and last so long because the area was plagued by driving winds, dry vegetation, and high temperatures. By the time it finally stopped burning, the Camp Fire had scorched 153,335 acres, about the size of Chicago. It had also destroyed more than fourteen thousand homes and killed eighty-five people. The number of birds and other animals that were killed remains unknown.

Thirteen-year-old Alexandria Villaseñor was visiting her family in Davis, California, during the Camp Fire. She and her mother, Kristin Hogue, had moved to New York City earlier in the year, but Villaseñor had come back to spend time with the rest of her family during the Thanksgiving break.

Although the fire was about eighty-five miles away, smoke blanketed the community. It also began seeping into the house where Villaseñor was staying. "That was very scary for me because I have asthma," she explained.

Villaseñor and her family rolled up wet towels and wedged them under doors and windows to try to stop the smoke from entering the house. They also made their own filters—the stores had sold out of them—to clean the dirty air that had made its way into the house. The face mask Villaseñor wore wasn't working well, so she held a wet washcloth over her mouth and nose. "My chest started to get prickly, as it does with asthma," she explained. "I felt like needles were pinching my chest." She worried she would be in serious danger if she spent much time outside. Ambulances zoomed by her family's house to pick up people who had collapsed because of the smoke.

Villaseñor and her family were so concerned about her worsening asthma that they agreed she should return to New York City earlier than planned. The homecoming was far from joyful. "She was really upset and angry when she got home," says her mother. "And sick for a few weeks." She even had to go the emergency room and visit with a pulmonologist, a doctor who specializes in the health of the lungs.

The Camp Fire was so deadly partly because of climate change...

During this difficult time, Villaseñor decided to study the conditions that made fires like the Camp Fire so dangerous. "I started to really research wildfires and I saw the connection between them and climate change," she explained. Scientists have linked some of the increase in the strength of wildfires to climate change, especially global warming.

The rise in our planet's average temperature has caused ice glaciers to melt, sea levels to rise, droughts to last longer, heat waves to grow hotter, and storms and fires to become more destructive. The Camp Fire was so deadly partly because of climate change: an unusually long drought in the area had dried out plants, bushes, and trees, making them burn more easily.

Scientists have also found that our planet's average temperature has climbed at a much faster pace in recent years than many experts thought it would. There are many reasons for this increase, but virtually all scientists agree that human activity is part of the cause. Not all human actions contribute to global warming, but it is clear that one activity is especially at fault: the burning of fossil fuels such as coal, oil, and natural gas.

. . . would the planet even exist in the years ahead?

Humans burn these fuels for the energy we need to run cars and trucks, factories and power plants, and homes and businesses. But burning fossil fuels is fraught with danger. It leads to the emission, or release, of gases into air surrounding our planet. These gases, often called "greenhouse gases," prevent heat from escaping our atmosphere. When this happens, the average temperature on Earth climbs. Scientists say that this trapped heat leads to global warming and all of its deadly consequences.

When Villaseñor saw the connection between climate change and wildfires, she resolved to take action. Her determination grew even stronger as she followed the news from the 2018 United Nations Climate Change Conference (COP24) in Poland. She hoped that the world leaders who were gathered there would agree to take concrete steps to reduce the release of greenhouse gases by 50 percent. Nothing like that happened. But Villaseñor was not discouraged by the news about COP24. On the contrary, she was inspired when she came across a video of a speech that climate activist Greta Thunberg had delivered at the conference.

Alexandria Villaseñor at the climate march in New York City on March 15, 2019.

Fifteen-year-old Thunberg had been invited to speak because she was the world's most visible activist for the climate. Thunberg first learned about climate change while she was in elementary school. One of her teachers showed a devastating video—starving polar bears, plastic garbage floating in the ocean, and extreme storms. The video made Thunberg cry and worry about the future.

As she remembers it, "My classmates were concerned when they watched the film, but when it stopped, they started thinking about other things. I couldn't do that. Those pictures were stuck in my head."

The terrible images led Thunberg to wonder whether she would have any future at all. If climate change was as bad as the scientists said, would the planet even exist in the years ahead? And if climate change was so serious, why weren't political leaders taking action to prevent it?

All of this churned inside her. "I kept that to myself because I'm not very much of a talker, and that wasn't healthy," she says. "I became very depressed and stopped going to school." Deep in depression, she stopped eating, too, and almost never spoke.

Her parents rearranged their work schedules so they could stay at home and take care of her. Thunberg was also diagnosed with Asperger syndrome. Asperger's made her super-focused in her studies and super-determined in her actions, but it also made it difficult for her to communicate with people. Sometimes she would say nothing, and other times her words would be shockingly blunt. Thunberg has said that for her, having Asperger's means she is "sometimes a bit different from the norm. And—given the right circumstances—being different is a superpower."

With help from medical professionals, Thunberg gradually began to express her thoughts and feelings to her parents. "I told them about my worries and concerns about the climate crisis and the environment," she says. "And it felt good just to get that off my chest."

At first, her parents assured her that everything would be okay and that she need not worry so much. But Thunberg was far from convinced, and she told them so. Using books and articles, graphs and reports, photos and documentaries, she taught her parents that they were wrong to believe that the future of the climate

"I decided enough was enough."

would be hopeful if people did not take drastic action to reduce the emissions of greenhouse gases. "And, after a while," she recalls, "they started listening to what I actually said."

They also changed their own behaviors. They installed solar panels, reduced their meat consumption, grew their own vegetables, and stopped flying in airplanes. Initially, they did this to help their daughter feel better, but over time, they came to embrace these practices.

Seeing her family change helped Thunberg come out of depression. "That's when I kind of realized I could make a difference," she explains. "And how I got out of that depression was that I thought: it is just a waste of time feeling this way because I can do so much good with my life."

In May 2018, Thunberg felt well enough to write an essay about climate change and submit it for publication. A Swedish newspaper published her essay, and shortly after, several climate activists contacted her about working together to raise awareness about the issue.

Inspired by the Marjory Stoneman Douglas High School students' activism for gun control, Thunberg suggested that they carry out a school strike to protest for

Greta Thunberg, bottom row, second from left, and Villaseñor, bottom row, third from right, joining other leaders at the New York City climate march on September 20, 2019.

the climate. The group chose not to do so, but Thunberg kept the idea front and center in her thoughts. Several months later, she announced to her parents that she would not be going back to school right away—instead, she would be carrying out a school strike for the climate.

"When school started in August this year," she wrote at the time, "I decided enough was enough. Sweden had just experienced its hottest summer ever. An election was coming up. No one was talking about climate change as an actual consequence of our life."

Fed up with inaction, Thunberg found a piece of wood and painted it with black letters, reading,

SKOLSTREJK FOR KLIMATET (SCHOOL STRIKE FOR CLI-
MATE). She also created a flyer with important facts
about the causes and effects of climate change.

On the morning of August 20, 2018, she put on her
blue hoodie, threw her backpack over her shoulders,
grabbed her sign, and hopped on her bike. Her des-
tination was an area just outside the Swedish parliament, the place where her country's political leaders
work. Thunberg wanted the politicians to see her sign,
read her flyer, and respond to her demand that Sweden
reduce emissions as much as other nations had agreed
to when they signed a pledge in 2015 called the Paris
Agreement.

Just outside parliament, Thunberg set up her sign
and sat next to it. No other activists joined her that day.
"I tried to bring people along to join me, but no one
was really interested, and so I had to do it by myself,"
she explained. "The first day, I sat alone from 8:30 a.m.
to 3:00 p.m.—the regular school day. And then on the
second day, people started joining me. And after that,
there were people there all the time."

These people included reporters from Sweden's
largest newspapers, as well as activists who took photos to post on social media. Before long, news about
Thunberg and her strike went viral on social media,
attracting attention from people around the globe.

After skipping school for three straight weeks,
Thunberg returned to the classroom, but every Friday,
she left to carry out her strike for the climate. News about
her strikes continued to spread on social media, with

people using the hashtag #FridaysForFuture to share updates. By the end of December, just four months after she began her campaign, more than twenty thousand students worldwide were striking with her every Friday, calling for politicians to reduce the emissions of greenhouse gases in their own countries.

Because of her international reputation, world leaders invited her to appear at an upcoming conference on the climate. On December 12, 2018, Thunberg delivered one of two speeches she gave at the COP24 conference in Poland. "I've learned that you are never too small to make a difference," she said, "and if a few children can get headlines all over the world just by not going to school, then imagine what we could all do together if we really wanted to."

But Thunberg was not hopeful about the leaders before her. "You are not mature enough to tell it like it is," she said. "Even that burden you leave to us children."

The stunned adults sat in silence as she continued. "You say you love your children above all else, and yet you're stealing their future in front of their very eyes. Until you start focusing on what needs to be done rather than what is politically possible, there is no hope."

It was time, she said, "to keep the fossil fuels in the ground."

"We have not come here to beg world leaders to care," she declared. "We have come here to let you know that change is coming, whether you like it or not. The real power belongs to the people!"

Villaseñor staging her weekly protest at a park bench near the United Nations headquarters in New York City.

Alexandria Villaseñor lit up when she watched Thunberg's speech. "She just put them in their place," she said. "That was extremely satisfying." It was also inspiring. After researching Thunberg and her story online, Villaseñor began to make concrete plans for her own school strike.

Villaseñor found some cardboard and made two signs. She painted SCHOOL STRIKE 4 CLIMATE on one and COP24 FAILED US on the other, and then she covered them with plastic to protect them from the weather. On December 14, 2018, she grabbed her signs, left her apartment with her mother, boarded the subway, and headed to the United Nations (UN) to begin her strike.

Villaseñor adopted Thunberg's method of striking because of its power to raise awareness. "Like Greta says, if people skip school, it gets the attention of everyone," she explained. "If just one person can do that, it gets the attention." And she picked the United Nations because of its unique identity and function. "I chose the United Nations headquarters because it's where the whole word comes together. It is where world leaders come to make big decisions."

Villaseñor was excited as she sat on the front steps to the UN with her signs next to her. This was her first-ever protest, and it was for a cause near and dear to her heart. When a UN security guard told her that she was not allowed to stay on the steps, "she got mad," her mother recalled. But Villaseñor quickly learned that she could sit on a nearby bench.

Satisfied with the new arrangement, she sat on that bench for four hours, a protest act that she has continued to repeat every Friday. She has endured all kinds of weather—rain, sleet, snow, even a polar vortex. With the temperature hovering around 10 degrees Fahrenheit on the eighth Friday of her strike, she zipped herself up in a heavy-duty sleeping bag.

From the beginning, Villaseñor's parents supported her decision to school-strike. "They understand my point of view," she said. "If I'm not going to have a future, then school won't matter, because we're going to be running from disasters." Her friends were initially confused by her actions. "At first when I started striking, they didn't really understand why it was important or why I was doing it. It was my job to educate them."

It took more than a month for another climate activist, thirty-one-year-old Stefanie Giglio, to join her at the United Nations. Villaseñor and her mother had been posting on social media, and major news outlets soon started to pay attention. In mid-February, the *Washington Post* published an article about her protest, and a few days later *CBS News* interviewed her on television. Many others soon followed with requests for interviews and photos.

When posting about her work, Villaseñor reached out to students who were interested in carrying out their own strikes. Working with twelve-year-old Haven Coleman of Colorado and sixteen-year-old Isra Hirsi of Chicago, the three activists founded US Youth Climate Strike. Their first major mission was to organize US students in every state for a worldwide school strike planned for March 15, 2019. Thunberg was the driving force behind the global strike.

"The idea is to collectively fight for our right to have a livable future," Coleman said at the time. When asked what she hoped the day would accomplish, Villaseñor replied: "I hope there are policies and laws put in place that will ensure we get down to where we lower emissions by fifty percent by 2030." She focused on the year 2030 because that is when many scientists believe that global warming will become irreversible.

The March 15 school strike, organized primarily through social media, turned out to be a massive global event. Organizers estimated that 1.4 million students skipped school in 123 countries to protest for the climate.

Protests occurred in about a dozen places across Manhattan, and Villaseñor set the tone for the day in

"Money won't matter when we're dead."

her first speech at the United Nations: "To those of you who deny the truth: we are ashamed of you," she declared. "That's why today the young people of the United States are declaring the era of American climate change denialism over."

NYC students gathered in several other locations, too—City Hall, the Bronx High School of Science, and Columbus Circle, among others—and while most protesters were from high schools, younger students also attended. In Washington Square Park, eight-year-old Eliza Schwartz spoke about her reason for striking: "Well, Mummy just has the news on after we get home and she's making dinner, and sometimes I'm so bored I just listen. I'm pretty sure I'll still be alive when the Earth will just like get destroyed from all this pollution and everything, so I just wanted to help."

All of the strikes featured signs like: DENIAL IS NOT A POLICY; MARCH FOR CLIMATE JUSTICE; CLIMATE CHANGE IS NOT A HOAX; MAKE OUR PLANET GREAT AGAIN; UNITE BEHIND THE SCIENCE; and FIGHT NOW OR SWIM L8R. Student demands also came through loud and clear in their chants: "Hey hey, ho ho! Climate change has got to go!"; "The Earth is dying! Stop denying!"; and "Climate change is not a lie! Do not let our planet die!"

Students marching down Market Street in the San Francisco Youth Climate Strike on March 15, 2019.

In the afternoon, a large group marched from Columbus Circle to the Museum of American History, where they met up with those who had protested in other parts of the city. The students then staged a die-in, lying down on the sidewalk and pretending to be dead. They wanted to show lawmakers that without reduced emissions of greenhouse gases, they would die. They chanted, "Money won't matter when we're dead," calling out politicians who favored business interests over the health of Planet Earth.

In addition to "dying," student protesters wore masks representing four politicians, President Trump and Senators Chuck Schumer, Dianne Feinstein, and Mitch McConnell. The students said these politicians were "fossils," too rigid and stuck in the past to support the drastic change required to halt climate change.

The March 15 strike was the largest ever staged by the global movement begun by Greta Thunberg. But Villaseñor, Thunberg, and other student activists remained dissatisfied because many world leaders still refused to take concrete steps to reduce emissions of greenhouse gases.

Ever persistent, Villaseñor continued her weekly strikes at the United Nations. She also joined in planning the second global climate strike, scheduled for May 24, 2019.

The second strike occurred in more than two thousand towns and cities in 125 countries. In New York City, students began a rowdy march that ended with a dramatic die-in at Times Square. The die-in featured eleven minutes of silence to draw attention to the eleven years left before global warming was predicted to become irreversible. Villaseñor took a video of the event and posted it on Twitter. Her simple caption read: "11 minutes of silence. 11 years to head off disaster. Times Square NYC die-in."

One day before the May 24 global strike, Villaseñor and forty-six other students, including Thunberg, published an article in the *Guardian*, a newspaper from London. The article served as an invitation to join another worldwide strike for the climate. This one would take place September 20, 2019, a few days before world leaders would be gathering in New York City for the United Nations Climate Action Summit.

A young activist changing the world in a protest at the Museum of American Natural History in New York City.

In the United States, the May 24 strike had fewer participants than the one on March 15. Villaseñor took the decline as a challenge and subsequently devoted more time to Earth Uprising—the non-profit organization she had founded. She created EU after she realized that many students were not protesting because they did not fully understand climate change and its dangerous consequences.

"Earth Uprising's main goal is to educate young people on climate change, to mobilize them to take direct actions," she explained. The organization does this by creating educational events and incorporating climate science into college curriculums. Busier than ever, Villaseñor continued to strike as she led Earth Uprising and planned the upcoming protest.

Climate activists from the Amazon marching in New York City on September 20, 2019.

For the September protest, the student organizers stressed the need for adults to participate. "We feel a lot of adults haven't quite understood that we young people won't hold off the climate crisis ourselves," the students wrote. "Sorry if this is inconvenient for you. But this is not a single-generation job. It's humanity's job."

The students were not surrendering their leadership of the movement. "But to change everything, we need everyone. It's time for us to unleash mass resistance—we have shown that collective action does work. We need to escalate the pressure [on political leaders] to make sure that change happens, and we must escalate together."

On Friday morning, September 20, 2019, Villaseñor put on her very own official strike T-shirt. It was bright

"... this is not a single-generation job. It's humanity's job."

green and read, NYC CORE COMMITTEE on the front and VILLASEÑOR on the back. There was no doubt that her black hiking boots were the right choice for the long day of marching that lay ahead.

Seven national youth-led groups—Earth Uprising, International Youth Council, Youth Climate Strike, Extinction Rebellion, Fridays for Future, Sunrise Movement, and Earth Guardians—had worked hard to get people to come protest. In countries in earlier time zones, the turnouts were already impressive. In Australia alone, three hundred thousand people had joined the strike. Reports of high numbers were also pouring in from Thailand, France, Germany, and South Africa.

In Foley Square in downtown Manhattan, a crowd of excited kids, teens, and adults gathered for the scheduled march to Battery Park. Many of the students were from New York City public schools. Because of pressure from Villaseñor and activist Xiye Bastida, city

237

school officials had decided to allow all NYC students to attend if they had permission from a parent or guardian. Elementary school students, of course, had to be accompanied by an adult.

Tens of thousands of students and adults streamed into Foley Square throughout the morning. The atmosphere was festive and bursting with energy.

A brief pre-march rally began around 12:30 p.m. One of the speakers was thirteen-year-old Marisol Rivera, whose family home had been wiped out by Hurricane Sandy in 2012. "I know there are people around the world who are suffering and are going through what I went through seven years ago," she said. "We can't leave people suffering. We all deserve to live free of fossil fuels and have a better life. This can happen to the people we know and care for. We all need to fight before it's too late."

Then, the crowd of marchers took off. Some of the marchers blew whistles, others beat drums, and lots of people danced along the way.

With a megaphone in her hand and a walkie-talkie strapped to her waist, Villaseñor positioned herself at the front of the march to make sure everything was okay—and to help lead the chants:

A better world is possible! We are unstoppable!

Sea levels are rising! And so are we!

What do we want? Climate justice! When do we want it? Now!

Seven national youth-led groups . . . had worked hard to get people to come protest.

Stop killing our future!

You had a future, and so should we!

We vote next!

She walked backward, looking at the crowd marching after her. She could see how cheerful, angry, and passionate her fellow marchers were. She also saw signs everywhere, with messages that were clear and colorful.

The marchers began streaming into Battery Park a little after 2:00 p.m., giving them enough time to rest and rehydrate before the 3:00 rally. As everyone hung out, Villaseñor granted interviews to reporters. In one of them, she explained the marchers' demands of the UN Climate Action Summit: eliminate the use of fossil fuels, organize a just transition to renewable energy, and hold major violators accountable for polluting the environment. "A lot of us are giving up our childhood," she added. "But we are giving up our childhood to have a future."

By the time the rally started, Battery Park was filled, completely filled, with about 250,000 climate strikers.

"This is the biggest climate strike ever in history . . ."

Most of them gathered in front of a stage with a screen showing the strikers' demands. At the top of the stage was a banner that read, WE ARE RISING TOO ~ CLIMATE STRIKE.

Like other march leaders, Villaseñor found a place next to the stage as the rally began. She clapped and cheered as speakers shared stories of the dangers of climate change, criticized negligent politicians, praised kids for taking leadership, and restated the strike's demands. But the highlight of the day was when she strode on stage, waved to the crowd, and took her place at the podium in front of the crowd of 250,000 people.

"Hi, everyone!" she said, with bright eyes and a brilliant smile. "How's it going?" The crowd cheered in reply. "I'm Alexandria Villaseñor, and this is my week 41 climate strike." Again, the crowd roared, and Villaseñor laughed before turning to her most important task of the day—introducing Thunberg.

Thunberg had also traveled to New York City for the march. She had sailed across the Atlantic from Plymouth, England, on a racing yacht powered only by wind, sun, and water. Boats typically use gas and oil, but Thunberg insisted on traveling in a way that was consistent with her opposition to the use of carbon fuels. After fifteen days at sea, the crew steered the emission-free

Leaders of the climate march in New York City, including Villaseñor, far left, on September 20, 2019.

boat into North Cove Marina in Manhattan. Young climate activists greeted Thunberg with waves and cheers.

"She is an icon of our time, and has been nominated for the Nobel Peace Prize," Villaseñor told the crowd. "And now she's here with us today. What I want to tell you about Greta Thunberg, though, is that she is the nicest, kindest, most humble person I ever met." The crowd erupted yet again, and Villaseñor and Thunberg shared a hug before the Swedish activist walked to center stage. She carried the sign she had been using since the first day of her strike.

"We will make them hear us!"

"Hello, New York City," Thunberg began. "Around the world today, about four million people have been striking. This is the biggest climate strike ever in history, and we all should be so proud of ourselves because we have done this together."

After praising the activists, she reminded them, as well as world leaders watching from afar, of the importance of the moment. "This Monday, world leaders will be gathered here, in New York City, for the United Nations Climate Action Summit. The eyes of the world will be on them. They have a chance to prove that they, too, are united behind the science. They have a chance to take leadership to prove that they actually hear us. Do you think they hear us?"

'No!" the crowd shouted in reply.

"We will make them hear us!" Thunberg responded. The protesters roared.

"We demand a safe future," she continued. "Is that really too much to ask?"

"No!"

"We are a wave of change. Together and united, we are unstoppable. This is what people power looks like. We will rise to the challenge. We will hold those who are most responsible for this crisis accountable. And we will make the world leaders act. We can, and we will!"

Despite the massive protests, the US government did not agree to take stronger action at the UN climate summit. According to the *New York Times*, "The United States, having vowed to pull out of the Paris Agreement, the pact among nations to jointly fight climate change, said nothing at all."

Still, Alexandria Villaseñor, Greta Thunberg, and other climate activists have refused to surrender. The protests go on. O

CHAPTER FOURTEEN

Marching for Dreamers

2019
*The student protesters begin
the march to the Supreme Court*

2010   2015   2020

Sixteen-year-old Valeria* put on a bright traffic vest. It wasn't especially fashionable, but it would serve the important function of identifying her as one of the event's main leaders. The only real problem with the ill-fitting garment was that it hid the powerful message on her T-shirt: UNSTOPPABLE, UNDENIABLE, UNDOCUMENTED, UNAFRAID.

Valeria had carefully prepared for this day. She had instructed her classmates at Benjamin Banneker Academic High School in Washington, DC: when it was time, they were to walk out of their classrooms, meet outside the school, and start the march to the Supreme Court of the United States. She had also explained the all-important reason for the protest: to demand that the Supreme Court rule in favor of Deferred Action for Childhood Arrivals (DACA).

DACA, a program created by a presidential order, has a controversial history. In December 2010, the US Senate failed to pass a bill called the Development, Relief and Education for Alien Minors (DREAM) Act. The purpose of the bill was to create a pathway to citizenship for undocumented immigrants who had been brought to the United States as children. People in this group often refer to themselves as Dreamers.

*To protect young people at risk of deportation, all activists' names in this chapter have been changed.

President Barack Obama was disappointed when the Senate did not pass the DREAM Act. On June 15, 2012, he signed and issued DACA, an executive memorandum, or presidential order, that protected about eight hundred thousand Dreamers from deportation—being sent back to the home country of their parents or caregivers. DACA also granted Dreamers permission to study and work in the United States.

Signing DACA was controversial because some political leaders and commentators believed that the president had overreached his authority. They said he had acted as a lawmaker, rather than as the executive leader of the country.

But Dreamers breathed a collective sigh of relief. Up to this point, their future had been unstable and uncertain. Law enforcement officers with US Immigration and Customs Enforcement (ICE) could have deported them without a moment's notice. Further, it had been difficult for many Dreamers to find jobs and schools willing to accept them. Dreamers did not enjoy the same rights and privileges that young citizens did.

"People are just breaking down and crying for joy when they [find] out what the president did," said Lorella at the time. She worked for United We Dream (UWD), an advocacy organization run by and for young people seeking constitutional rights for Dreamers and their families.

Nevertheless, there were limits to the celebrations. DACA did not grant Dreamers citizenship, nor did it build a path for them to become citizens. While

DACA did not grant Dreamers citizenship, nor did it build a path for them to become citizens.

Dreamers were pleased with what DACA had accomplished, they continued to protest for the right to gain citizenship—for themselves and for older undocumented immigrants. On July 10, 2013, UWD organized about five hundred Dreamers and their family members for a citizenship ceremony near the US Capitol. The protesters recited the Pledge of Allegiance, sang "The Star-Spangled Banner," and swore an oath penned especially for the day: "I hereby pledge to live out the highest values of this land. I am the future of this nation. I am the American dream."

Two months later, Dreamers sat in the way of a bus that was planning to deport immigrants in Phoenix, Arizona. Nearby, more than one hundred other protesters encircled an ICE building. Ray, a UWD leader, was arrested during the protest. "I am so fed up with people playing games with our lives," he explained.

In the following months and years, UWD and other pro-immigrant groups organized many more protests, including courageous acts of civil disobedience. But none of it worked. The unstable lives of Dreamers took a turn for the worse on September 5, 2017, when President Donald Trump stated that his administration

247

would phase out DACA beginning in March 2018. Dreamers could face immediate deportation to their family's home country.

United We Dream responded to the president's announcement by staging nonviolent protests demanding that Congress pass legislation protecting Dreamers. But Congress was controlled by Republicans, who supported the president's position. They refused to back the Dreamers' demands.

Meanwhile, immigrant rights organizations and their allies also mounted a legal challenge to Trump's decision, and several federal courts blocked the termination of DACA. But the Trump administration appealed to the US Supreme Court, asking the justices to overturn the decisions of the lower courts. The Supreme Court agreed to consider the appeal, and on November 12, 2019, the justices heard oral arguments for and against the repeal of DACA.

Four days before these oral arguments took place, Valeria and her peers walked out of their classrooms at Benjamin Banneker Academic High School. It was a gorgeous, sunny day, but the morning was cool enough for Valeria to wear her beanie over her ears. The air was so crisp, many of the marchers wore their own T-shirts— printed with UNSTOPPABLE, UNDENIABLE, UNDOCU- MENTED, UNAFRAID—over their sweatshirts and jackets.

A Dreamer speaking in front of butterfly signs; the butterfly is a symbol of the freedom to migrate.

Valeria held a white megaphone, with a bumper sticker on it that read, RESIST DEPORTATIONS, waiting for the right moment to begin the march.

The student protesters began the march to the Supreme Court. Many of the students held signs, some of them handmade and some made by United We Dream and the other sponsoring organizations. They read: HOME IS HERE; NO HUMAN IS ILLEGAL; DEFEND DACA; IMMIGRANTS MAKE AMERICA GREAT.

It was not a quiet march, especially as the Capitol and the Court came into view. Parading down tree-lined streets, the students bellowed out one chant after another:

Dreamers and their allies marching to the US Supreme Court.

D-A! D-A! DACA, DACA's here to stay!

Up, up with liberation! Down, down with deportation!

The people united! Will never be divided!

Here to stay! Here to stay!

Say it loud! Say it clear! Immigrants are welcome here!

Sometimes the marchers switched from English to Spanish. One of the favorite chants came from the migrant farmworkers movement in the 1960s: "*¡Si, se puede! ¡Si, se puede!* Yes, we can! Yes, we can!"

"I'm here today because I'm tired of having an uncertain future."

Banneker students then joined hundreds of other high school and university students—about ten schools were represented—for a rally in a public park near the Supreme Court. As bolts of enthusiasm pinged through the growing crowd, Sam, a student from Trinity Washington University, gave a quiet interview to a reporter. "I'm here today because I'm tired of having an uncertain future," he said. "I'm tired of being in limbo, and I'm ready for a permanent solution for DACA . . . I want to pursue my dreams and become a doctor, and without DACA, I cannot do that."

A short time later, the crowd of about 725 students erupted in cheers when Claudia, an organizer from United We Dream, welcomed everyone to the rally. The first student speaker was Gabriel, from DC International School. He said that because he was the son of immigrants, he knew how "essential" they were to the nation. "If immigrants were not here, the nation would not be what it is."

Then, it was Valeria's turn, and as she stepped onto the park bench to make her speech, she beamed. "I'm really excited and happy," she said. "This is my first time leading a school walkout." The crowd cheered her on as she read her speech from her phone.

I want to start off by saying I am the daughter of immigrants. My mother was born in Bolivia and came to the U.S. with a work visa. My father is from El Salvador. He came to the U.S. in 2001, after a drastic earthquake impacted his hometown. Both of my parents came here full of hope that they would have a better lifestyle, a place to call home.

I am here today because I want to ensure a pathway to citizenship for all DACA recipients, for people with TPS [Temporary Protected Status] in our immigrant community.

Home is here! My parents deserve to be here. They should not have to live in fear every day. We [could be] separated from our family at any moment. The fear of losing everything they have worked so hard for . . .

At this point, Valeria had to stop and take a breath. "I'm shaking," she said loudly enough for others to hear. The students cheered her on. "Keep going!" they shouted. "Keep going."

Valeria began again: "This country is run by immigrants. They deserve to be here."

The crowd roared when Valeria wrapped up her speech. As she stepped down from the bench, still shaking, Claudia hopped back up and asked the protesters to repeat a chant she would lead.

Relieved to be back among her friends, Valeria grabbed her megaphone, held it up to her mouth, tilted her head back, and shouted out the new chant: "It is our duty to fight for our freedom. It is our duty to win.

Activists with signs sharing the march's theme.

We must love and protect one another. We have nothing to lose but our chains."

Several more students gave speeches and pep talks, including Vanessa from Woodrow Wilson High School, who said, "Make your voices heard today! Our voice—the youth voice—is so important. So be loud today! Be so loud!"

The students happily took her advice as they left the park and marched to the Supreme Court Building. "Undocumented!" they shouted. "Unafraid!"

Leading the way was a dark banner carried by five girls. It read, UNITED WE DREAM, and depicted three young immigrant activists—a boy holding a mega-phone; another boy with a fist thrust into the air; and between them, a tall girl standing defiantly, with her hands on her hips. Following the banner were ten girls carrying ten signs—each painted with a monarch but-terfly, the symbol of migration and freedom.

Behind the butterfly signs was the large group of students determined to let the Supreme Court Justices know who they were and what they wanted. One of the chants they used was adopted from cheerleaders across the nation:

> Everywhere we go
> People want to know
> Who we are
> So we tell them.

> We are the immigrants,
> The mighty, mighty immigrants,
> Fighting for justice,
> Fighting for DACA!

As the students gathered in front of the Supreme Court Building, their voices grew louder. "Whose house?" a student leader yelled. "Our house!" the crowd belted.

The ten girls holding butterfly signs made a place for themselves right in front of the Court's majestic steps. On each of the ten butterfly paintings was a letter, and when the girls spread out in order, their butterfly signs read, H-E-R-E-T-O-S-T-A-Y.

Still holding her megaphone, Valeria smiled when she saw the sign. Like everyone else there that day, she could see that high above the protesters, engraved on the façade of the Supreme Court Building, was a phrase indicating the purpose of the Court's work: EQUAL JUSTICE UNDER LAW.

Those four words were exactly why they were there—to secure "equal justice under law" for Dreamers and all undocumented immigrants. That simple yet profound phrase represented their unfulfilled dream of dreams.

On June 18, 2020, the Supreme Court ruled that the Trump administration may not immediately end DACA. The 5-4 decision came as a surprise to many DACA recipients.

A Dreamer named Jesus said, "I've been on the edge the past few months, just kind of worried to death about what the Supreme Court decision was going to be. A lot of my activist friends and a lot of people who are involved in immigrant rights . . . [were] preparing us for the worst, so I'm relieved."

But there was a chance the relief might not last. After the decision, the Trump administration began discussing other ways to eliminate DACA.

Whatever happens next, Jesus, Ana, and Dreamers everywhere will no doubt continue to fight—for the right to say, "Home is here." O

The George Floyd Protests

2020
*Minneapolis police
officers kill George Floyd*

2010   2015   2020

"**A**s a Black girl, I am scared," said teenager Jade Ofotan. "Being a Black person in this country and watching George Floyd being murdered in broad daylight was terrible. Every day that I step out of the house I worry for myself and my family. I don't want that to be a problem anymore for POC [people of color] in America."

On May 25, 2020, Minneapolis police officers arrested George Floyd for allegedly using a counterfeit twenty-dollar bill at a convenience store. During the arrest, three police officers pinned him to the ground. One of them, white officer Derek Chauvin, put his knee on Floyd's neck.

Floyd begged Chauvin to get off, telling the officers repeatedly, "I can't breathe."

By the time he stood up, Chauvin had knelt on Floyd's neck for a total of eight minutes and forty-six seconds—and Floyd was dead.

Videos of the arrest, taken by bystanders, soon traveled across social media, sparking horror, sadness, and fury.

After Minneapolis Police Chief Medaria Arradondo watched the video, he fired the three officers as well as another who had stood by and watched during the arrest. But the officers were not immediately charged with a crime.

Protests erupted throughout the country. Many of the demonstrations centered on police stations and government buildings. In Washington, DC, thousands of people filled Lafayette Park, just across the street from the White House.

"Black lives matter!" and "No justice, no peace!" were two of the more popular chants. Though some of the protests turned violent, most were peaceful vigils, rallies, and marches.

Early on, the protesters had two main demands: the arrest of those responsible for Floyd's death, and the end of police brutality against people of color.

On May 29, Chauvin was arrested and charged with murder and manslaughter. Several days later, the three other officers were arrested and charged with aiding and abetting the murder.

Shayla Avery, a student at Berkeley High School in California, was paying close attention to the news. She was upset that at least some of her teachers were not addressing the protests.

"We should do something," she texted her friend.

They did.

Avery and two friends, Hadassah Zenor-Davis and Ultraviolet Schneider-Dwyer, began to organize a march in their Berkeley community. The students wanted their march to protest the murders of George

March organizers Shayla Avery and Ultraviolet Schneider-Dwyer wearing masks to prevent the spread of Covid-19.

Floyd and all other Black men and women unjustly killed by police officers and racists. The list of victims they had in mind included Breonna Taylor, a twenty-six-year-old emergency room technician who, though unarmed and innocent of any crime, was shot eight times by police officers in Louisville, Kentucky, in March 2020. Until that point, her murder had not been acknowledged on a national scale.

"We are standing in solidarity with lives like George Floyd and Breonna Taylor and so many others," Schneider-Dwyer told the *Daily Californian*, a student-run newspaper.

She added that the march would also advocate for educational course changes at Berkeley High School and the Berkeley Unified School District. "Teachers need to be taught how to talk about racism in their classes," Schneider-Dwyer explained. "We need more education about Black history and Black leaders in all grades. Showing our alliance with (Black students) is the most important thing we can do."

The student leaders named their protest the Stand with Black Youth March. They called upon school administrators to train teachers in racism and anti-racism, combat school segregation, and expand the number of courses about Black history, culture, and social issues.

"We need young children to be educated on these things for the rest of their lives," Schneider-Dwyer said.

The leaders used social media platforms, friendly community groups, and print media to share their announcement about the march:

Berkeley High School Students are organizing a nonviolent, peaceful rally and march on Tuesday, June 9th, in solidarity with George Floyd, Breonna Taylor, Ahmaud Arbery, Sandra Bland, Nina Pop, Tony McDade, Michael Brown, Eric Garner, Tamir Rice, Trayvon Martin, Alton Sterling, Oscar Grant, and all of the wrongly taken Black lives from police brutality—and to protest against the systems and institutions that feed into the systemic racism so deeply rooted in our society. We're protesting the lack of acknowledgment of Black history, the Black reality and overall the Black community in schools. Why doesn't anybody teach us about our history? Why aren't we taught what's REALLY out in the world for us? We have come together to highlight the injustices that Black youth face in schools along within society itself.

A portrait of George Floyd led the protest march.

News about the march spread fast as Avery, Zenor-Davis, and Schneider-Dwyer focused on planning the details. They lined up drummers, rented a large truck to carry some of the participants, found a sound system and someone to run it, painted signs, talked to reporters, coordinated with other protest groups, and organized adult helpers. Because of the ongoing COVID-19 pandemic, the three leaders also made sure that marchers wore protective masks.

On June 9, 2020, hundreds of people arrived at San Pablo Park for the 4:00 p.m. start of the march.

Zenor-Davis smiled as she surveyed the large—and diverse—crowd. "This isn't just Black kids," she said. "I feel unity. I feel like this isn't just my fight, like other people want to see the same results I want to see . . . I feel a real big sense of community right now. I'm very proud of my community for coming out: different races, ethnicities."

A large truck with banners, drummers, and organizers leading the march.

Nearby was a bright yellow truck with a trailer bed large enough to hold about twenty-five people. Excited students swarmed around it, decorating it with signs that read BLACK LIVES MATTER; STAND WITH BLACK YOUTH; and NATIVES IN SOLIDARITY.

Berkeley students wanted their local community leaders to shift a portion of tax dollars from police budgets to social programs that would support high-quality education, health care, jobs, and housing—the key ingredients to a vibrant, flourishing, peaceful community. Another sign on the truck spoke to this, reading, DEFUND POLICE TERROR, INVEST IN PEOPLE'S POWER.

As everyone else milled about, preparing for the start of the march, a group of about forty drummers swayed to their own beats. Students smiled and danced.

"We are lifting up the Black youth, the voices of the Black youth."

Though they were angry, this was also a time for the marchers to celebrate solidarity, being together in their fight for racial justice.

Zenor-Davis spoke to a local news reporter. "We're really trying to get our message out there," she explained. "Both our criminal justice system and our school system have not been set up for Black youth. We want to shed light on that, and show how similar the two systems really are, and change that."

In the crowd, a young white woman wore a T-shirt that read, I'M ROOTING FOR EVERYBODY BLACK, while a young Black woman handed out free snacks and water. Parents held the hands of their children, and high schoolers gathered in circles of friends, chatting and laughing. The woodsy smell of burning sage filled the air.

Zenor-Davis, Avery, and Schneider-Dwyer climbed on top of the truck bed and used the speaker system to address the crowd.

"We are lifting up the Black youth, the voices of the Black youth," Schneider-Dwyer announced. "If you are a Black young person in this crowd right now, there is space for you to say your piece, whether it's the school, the justice system, or just being Black in America . . .

We're opening the door for the conversation in Berkeley, because it was too quiet before."

As the speeches ended, Zenor-Davis, standing at the back of the truck, now filled with drummers and students, yelled to the crowd, "Are you ready?"

And with those words, she began to chant: "Ain't no power but the power of youth, and the power of youth don't stop!"

The crowd joined in, the drummers began beating, and the truck took off. About eight hundred people followed. Skateboarders and bicyclists, as well as adults on foot, also helped to lead the way from San Pablo Park to Berkeley High School.

It was a joyful, peaceful march with a lot of chanting: "Black lives matter!" "George Floyd! Breonna Taylor!" "No justice, no peace!" "Hey hey, ho ho! These racist cops have got to go!"

A painted portrait of George Floyd was displayed at the front of the truck along with a sign that read, SOLIDARITY FROM THE BAY 2 MINNEAPOLIS.

At the high school, the drummers formed a circle, a long-recognized sign of a peaceful protest, and a handful of marchers danced inside it. Then the drummers and marchers fell silent for eight minutes and forty-six seconds, the exact time that Chauvin had knelt on Floyd's neck.

Eight minutes and forty-six seconds of complete silence.

Some protesters took a knee and raised their fists in solidarity with Floyd. Some held signs reading, I CAN'T BREATHE. And some cried.

"I can't breathe"—some of the last words spoken by Floyd—appeared on numerous protest signs at the march.

As the silence came to an end, the drums beat again, and protesters moved to the brick-paved street directly in front of the high school. There, they painted *Black Lives Matter* in giant yellow letters on the street, a lasting sign of the march and its mission.

High school and college students, as well as adults, led similar marches across the country, in every state and the District of Columbia, and not just in major cities and suburbs, but also in small towns and rural areas not accustomed to marches for racial justice. Because of this, the George Floyd protests quickly became the broadest ever in US history, touching millions upon millions of lives. They spread across the globe, too. Black Lives Matter marches took place in South Africa, Brazil, South

Organizers Hadassah Zenor-Davis, left, Ultraviolet
Schneider-Dwyer, center, and Shayla Avery leading
chants from the back of the truck.

Korea, Switzerland, Hong Kong, Australia, France, Spain,
Belgium, the United Kingdom, and other countries.

George Floyd had touched the world.

And the protests brought changes throughout the
nation.

Some police departments banned the use of choke
holds and other neck restraints when arresting people.
Mayors and police chiefs in major cities formed working groups to develop better policies for using force
and policing communities of color. Others wrote rules
requiring officers to intervene if they see a colleague
using excessive force.

The protests also resulted in changes far beyond
police departments. Some companies announced
changes to the names and images of products that per-
petuated harmful stereotypes of Black people. PepsiCo,
for example, said that it would remove "Aunt Jemima"
from its pancake syrup and mix packages. The original

image portrayed "Aunt Jemima" as a happy enslaved woman. The name and the character were taken from early minstrel shows—plays in which white actors appeared in blackface and ridiculed Black people. The Aunt Jemima brand enforced the stereotype of the happy "mammy"—a Black woman who cooked and cleaned for white families, and even raised their children, content despite her oppressive circumstances. Other companies fired leaders and employees who had expressed racism in words or actions.

Streaming media platforms removed films with racist messages. NASCAR banned the Confederate flag at its races. The National Football League commissioner, who had previously refused to support protests for racial justice, stated the NFL would encourage peaceful demonstrations. Majority-white communities began to celebrate Juneteenth, a holiday marking the emancipation of slaves. And high school and college administrators laid plans to improve the way they teach about racism, and how they serve Black students and other students of color.

Whether these changes will make a significantly safer world for people of color remains to be seen. They are the first steps in a long journey, and many protesters continue to call for bigger, more substantial reforms. But in these protests we have seen the passion of a generation who will fight tirelessly in defense of racial justice and Black lives.

When the system or government fails, students will once again take up the charge—and march! ○

Tips for Marching

If there is a cause you care about that you want to bring to the attention of your community—or the nation—a great way to do that is to march. Like the kids in this book, you can stand tall and stride forward for peace, freedom, and justice for all. Whether you attend a march or decide to organize your own, here are some tips to help you make the most of the experience for yourself and your cause.

📣 Before the March 📣

Ask yourself,

1.

What are the social issues or problems I care most about?

2.

Why are these important to me?

3.

Do I feel so strongly that I would march for them?

4.

Do I know the risks of marching in this event?

5.

Am I willing to accept these risks?

6.

Whom can I ask about all this?

7.

With whom can I attend the march?

- Find an existing march that fights for a cause you support. Learn as much about the march and its organizers as you can to confirm that it matches your values.

- If there's no march for the issue you want to highlight, organize your own!

- Obtain your parents' permission, if possible.

📣 If You're the Organizer 📢

- In addition to the tips here, consult at least several online guides for organizing a march. They offer step-by-step instructions about all the details you'll need to address.

- **Ask for help!** Experienced protesters can offer advice and resources to help you prepare to march.

- Assign roles to those who want to help. Make sure someone takes care of securing any permits or insurance that might be required by law. Ask others to help arrange for sound equipment, first aid stations, and fundraising.

- Simplify your message into a short march title—for example: **Kids for Free Speech!**

- Formulate one or two main goals—for example, the passage of a new law, the repeal of a harmful one, the hiring or firing of a certain leader.

- Identify the people in power who can make the decisions you're seeking. You'll need to direct your message to them.

- Choose the best time for your march. Weekend and late-morning or early-afternoon marches often allow for the most attendance.

- Pick the most appropriate location. Is there a place that symbolizes your cause? A particular building where decision-makers gather?

- **Share!** Use one-on-one conversations and social media to announce your plans and connect with interested family members, friends, neighbors, and groups.

- **Publicize!** Send details about the march to newspapers and radio and television stations.

📢 For Everyone 📢

- Make and carry a personal ID with your name, address, phone number, and emergency contact phone numbers.

- Check rules about what you may and may not take to the march.

- Make signs, buttons, T-shirts, flags, or banners. **Be creative and express yourself!** Signs are a great way to make your voice ring out farther and louder than you can shout. They also help show the diversity of voices that are part of the cause. Go all out, but remember, the clearer and more easily understandable your sign is, the more impact it will have.

- Create a petition to send to political leaders. It can start by stating, **"We demand . . ."**

- Make colorful, informative flyers to distribute to spectators. Carefully explain the reasons for the march, using statistics when you can.

- Memorize your favorite protest chants or **make up your own!**

- **Get a good night's sleep!**

📢 Day of the March 📢

- Wear clothes that match the weather, as well as comfortable shoes that are appropriate for long walks.

- Pack water, nutritious snacks, your ID, phone, phone charger, camera, and only the money you'll need.

- **Don't forget your signs or other protest items!**

- **At the march, have fun!**

- Use the buddy system, marching with family members or one or more friends.

- Identify the location of bathrooms, first-aid stations, march helpers, and law enforcement officials.

- Find your place. Pay special attention to places where other kids have gathered, or find another spot in the crowd where you will feel comfortable marching.

- Join in the singing and chanting.

- Avoid protesters or counterprotesters who make you feel uncomfortable in any way.

- Talk to *peaceful* protesters and counterprotesters.

- **Take lots of pictures and videos!** You'll want to remember the day and your presence there. Photos and videos can also showcase and increase a march's impact even after it's completed.

- **Stay hydrated and eat!**

- If there's a rally, try to get close to the stage.

- Leave when you want to leave.

📣 After the March 📣

- Evaluate your experience. **Did you have a good time? Would you want to go again?** Ask yourself deeper questions, too, such as, **"What did our march accomplish?"** And, **"Was it worth all the effort?"**

- Share your experiences, positive and negative, with friends and family.

- Write down anything you wish you had done or brought to this march, or that you would want to have for the next one.

- Plan your next steps for creating change, such as writing to a school or government leader.

- **Remember—you did it!**

Acknowledgments

During my research for this book, I often found tears welling in my eyes as I read about ordinary kids who demonstrated extraordinary courage in their marches for peace, freedom, and justice. I thank all the kid marchers throughout US history for their fierce commitment to building a better world for all of us.

John Rudolph of Dystel, Goderich & Bourret LLC, deserves my deepest gratitude for believing in this project early on, helping me reshape and sharpen it, and finding the right home for it.

Elise Howard, founding editor and publisher of Algonquin Young Readers, and her colleague, editor Sarah Alpert, improved my original manuscript in ways I could never have imagined; so did Ashley Mason, Laura Williams, Kayla Escobedo, Susan Wilkins, and Emma Hager. I am honored to work with them, and deeply grateful for their vision, creativity, and style.

Many thanks, too, to Sharon Stetler Herr for proofreading parts of the manuscript, and especially for her friendship these last twenty years.

I reserve my utmost thanks for my family—Karin, Jackson, and Nate—for their love upon love, their interest in equal justice under law, and their willingness to jump in the car and head to another march.

Notes

INTRODUCTION

"Today, we march": Founders of March for Our Lives, *Glimmer of Hope: How Tragedy Sparked a Movement* (New York: RAZORBILL and Dutton, 2018), 164.

"freaking out": Founders, *Glimmer of Hope*, 162.

"We know what we want": Founders, *Glimmer of Hope*, 164.

"WHAT DO YOU LIKE MORE": Lisa Ryan, "The Most Inspiring Signs from the March for Our Lives," *The Cut*, March 24, 2018, thecut.com.

"I have a dream": Nick Penzenstadler, "March for Our Lives: Martin Luther King, Jr.'s Granddaughter Has Dream 'Enough Is Enough,'" *USA Today*, March 24, 2018.

CHAPTER 1

"WE ONLY ASK FOR JUSTICE": "Mother Jones Arrives," *The New York Times*, July 24, 1903; and Russell E. Smith, "The March of the Mill Children," *Social Science Review* 41.3 (September 1967): 301.

"All around my house": Elliott J. Gorn, *Mother Jones: The Most Dangerous Woman in America* (New York: Hill and Wang, 2001), 41-42.

"I would look out": Gorn, *Mother Jones*, 42.

"Every day little children": Mary Harris Jones, *The Autobiography of Mother Jones* (Chicago: Charles H. Kerr & Company, 1925), chap. 10, digital.library.upenn.edu.

"One of these boys": "Textile Strikes in Silent March," *The Philadelphia Inquirer*, June 5, 1903.

"From time to time": Jones, *Autobiography*, chap. 10.

"We ask you, Mr. President": Mother Jones, letter to Theodore Roosevelt, July 15, 1903, in *Mother Jones Speaks: Speeches and Writings of a Working-Class Fighter*, ed. Philip S. Foner (Atlanta, GA: Pathfinder Press, 1983), 713.

"That night we camped": Jones, *Autobiography*, chap. 10.

"We want President Roosevelt": "Mother Jones Speaks to Coney Island Crowd," *The New York Times*, July 27, 1903.

CHAPTER 2

"PORTLAND BONUS MARCH": Paul Dickson and Thomas B. Allen, "Marching on History: When a 'Bonus Army' of World War I Veterans Converged on Washington, MacArthur, Eisenhower and Patton Were There to Meet Them," *Smithsonian Magazine*, February 2003, smithsonian.com.

"I remember when we saw": Paul Dickson and Thomas B. Allen, *The Bonus Army: An American Epic* (New York: Walker & Company, 2004), 114. This chapter's account of the Oliver family is indebted to Dickson and Allen's work.

"got one dollar": Dickson and Allen, *The Bonus Army*, 114.

"Prepare yourselves for disappointment": John D. Weaver, "Bonus March," *American Heritage* 14.4 (1963), americanheritage.com.

"all suffering Americans": Lucy G. Barber, *Marching on Washington: The Forging of an American Political Tradition* (Berkeley, CA: University of California Press, 2002), 93.

"All you could do": Dickson and Allen, *The Bonus Army*, 115.
"Come on! Come on!": Dickson and Allen, *The Bonus Army*, 180.
"Had the President not acted today": Dickson and Allen, "Marching on History," February 2003.

CHAPTER 3

"I'm sick and tired": Teri Kanefield, *The Girl from the Tarpaper School: Barbara Rose Johns and the Advent of the Civil Rights Movement* (New York: Abrams Books for Young Readers, 2014), 6. For many of Johns's quotations, Kanefield drew from Barbara Johns, untitled memoir, no date, Barbara Johns Papers, Robert Russa Moton Museum, Farmville, Virgnia.

"chicken coops": "Barbara Johns Leads Prince Edward County Student Walkout," no date, SNCC Digital Gateway, snccdigital.org.

"Then there were the smells": John A. Stokes, *Students on Strike: Jim Crow, Civil Rights, Brown, and Me* (Washington, DC: National Geographic, 2008), 50.

"the only person": Edwilda Allen, interviewed by George Gilliam and Mason Mills of the Ground Beneath Our Feet Project, 2000, Virginia Center for Digital History, University of Virginia, vcdh.virginia.edu.

"Why don't you do something": Denise M. Watson, "Barbara Johns Day Honors Student Whose Walkout Contributed to Landmark Desegregation Case," *The Virginian-Pilot*, April 22, 2018.

"Right then and there": Kanefield, *The Girl from the Tarpaper School*, 10.
"As I lay in bed that night": Kanefield, *The Girl from the Tarpaper School*, 12.
"If they can do that": *Times-Dispatch* Staff, "Ex-Principal M. Boyd Jones Dies," *Richmond Times-Dispatch*, January 23, 2008.

"It was about a quality education": "Barbara Johns of Farmville, Virginia," video segment of *The Rise and Fall of Jim Crow*, documentary, Quest Productions, Videoline Productions, and Educational Broadcasting Corporation, 2002, pbslearningmedia.org.

"We wanted so much here": Joe Buber, "The 16-Year-Old Who Fought Segregation," *The New York Times Upfront*, April 22, 2019, upfront.scholastic.com.
"We were taught": Kanefield, *The Girl from the Tarpaper School*, 21.
"We called our secret plan": Stokes, *Students on Strike*, 56.
"We had to get him off campus": "Barbara Johns of Farmville, Virginia," *The Rise and Fall of Jim Crow*, 2002.
"Would you please come down": "Barbara Johns of Farmville, Virginia," *The Rise and Fall of Jim Crow*, 2002.
"We were packed": Stokes, *Students on Strike*, 65.
"What is going on": "Barbara Johns of Farmville, Virginia," *The Rise and Fall of Jim Crow*, 2002.
"This is for the students": Watson, "Barbara Johns Day Honors Student Whose Walkout Contributed to Landmark Desegregation Case," *The Virginian-Pilot*, April 22, 2018.
"We have to make a change": "Barbara Johns of Farmville, Virginia," *The Rise and Fall of Jim Crow*, 2002.
"What's going to happen to us": "Barbara Johns of Farmville, Virginia," *The Rise and Fall of Jim Crow*, 2002.

"What if they put us in jail": Watson, "Barbara Johns Day Honors Student Whose Walkout Contributed to Landmark Desegregation Case," April 22, 2018.

"Strike the school": "Barbara Johns of Farmville, Virginia," *The Rise and Fall of Jim Crow*, 2002.

"Two bits, four bits": Stokes, *Students on Strike*, 65.

"Don't be afraid": "Eyewitness to Jim Crow: Joan Johns Cobb Remembers," *Congress of Racial Equality*, no date, core-online.org.

"Down with tarpaper shacks": Ronald L. Heinemann, "Moton School Strike and Prince Edward County School Closings," *Encyclopedia Virginia*, January 21, 2014, encyclopediavirginia.org.

"People would hear us": Lance Booth, "Overlooked No More: Barbara Johns, Who Defied Segregation in Schools," *The New York Times*, May 8, 2019.

"She wanted us to take her case": Booth, "Overlooked No More," May 8, 2019.

"Due to the fact": Kanefield, *The Girl from the Tarpaper School*, 26.

"Carrie typed it up": Stokes, *Students on Strike*, 70.

"You upstarts!": "Barbara Johns of Farmville, Virginia," *The Rise and Fall of Jim Crow*, 2002.

"Initially, nobody dared dream": Booth, "Overlooked No More," May 8, 2019.

"The problem is that a new colored high school": Kanefield, *The Girl from the Tarpaper School*, 32.

"Don't let any Tom, Dick, or Harry Pervall": Katy June-Friesen, "Massive Resistance in a Small Town: Before and After *Brown* in Prince Edward County, Virginia," *Humanities* 34.5 (September/October 2013), neh.gov.

"We had tears": Stokes, *Students on Strike*, 98-99.

"In the field of public education": Luther A. Huston, "1896 Ruling Upset," *The New York Times*, May 18, 1954.

"In seeing an injustice": Gregory S. Schneider, "Virginia Dedicates State Office Building in Honor of Civil Rights Pioneer," *The Washington Post*, February 23, 2017.

CHAPTER 4

"My mother had told me": Denise Stewart, "Children's March 1963: A Defiant Moment," *The Root*, May 1, 2013, theroot.com.

"We cannot in all good conscience": "Birmingham Campaign," *King Encyclopedia*, no date, The Martin Luther King, Jr. Research and Education Institute, kinginstitute. stanford.edu.

"D-Day" and "the party in the park": *Mighty Times: The Children's March*, HBO documentary, produced and directed by Robert Hudson, 2004.

"'Daddy,' the boy said": *The Autobiography of Martin Luther King, Jr.*, ed. Clayborne Carson (New York: Warner Books, 2001), 207.

"Where had these writers": Carson, *Autobiography*, 206.

"The children understood the stakes": Carson, *Autobiography*, 207.

"The reality of it": *Mighty Times: The Children's March*, 2004.

"It's Time!": *Mighty Times: The Children's March*, 2004.

"At one school, the principal": Carson, *Autobiography*, 208.

"We poured into Sixteenth Street": *Mighty Times: The Children's March*, 2004.

"Segregation is a sin": Steven Levingston, "Children Have Changed America Before, Braving Fire Hoses and Police Dogs for Civil Rights," *The Washington Post*, March 23, 2018.

"Ain't gonna let nobody": Freeman A. Hrabowski, "Bull Connor Spat in My Face: The Civil Rights March That Changed Me Forever," *Salon*, January 18, 2016, salon.com.

"Are they okay?" and "Will they be safe?": Carson, *Autobiography*, 233.

"He couldn't even say freedom": *Mighty Times: The Children's March*, 2004.

"Don't worry about your children": Carson, *Autobiography*, 211.

"The heart of the question": "Transcript of the President's Address," *The New York Times*, June 12, 1963.

"They are acting not out of": "Transcript of the President's Address," June 12, 1963.

"Looking back, it is clear": Carson, *Autobiography*, 206.

CHAPTER 5

"Gentleman, everything is going": Jervis Anderson, *Bayard Rustin: Troubles I've Seen* (New York: HarperCollins, 1997), 255.

"Five, six, seven, eight": *I Must Resist: Bayard Rustin's Life in Letters*, ed. Michael G. Long (San Francisco: City Lights Books, 2012), 212.

"We were going to shut down the city": Sondra Barrett Hassan, interviewed by Kelly Navies, October 9, 2013, OHP 24, March on Washington 50th Anniversary Oral History Project, DC Public Library, Special Collections.

"No, Rustin is Mr. March-on-Washington": John D'Emilio, *Lost Prophet: The Life and Times of Bayard Rustin* (New York: Free Press, 2003), 347.

"Ain't nobody gonna stop me": "I'm Marching Down Freedom Road," words by Langston Hughes, music by Emerson Harper, 1942 recording. See "That's Why We're Marching: WWII and the American Folk Song Movement," Smithsonian/Folkways, 1996, folkways.si.edu.

"I know all of us are going": Frank C. Girardot and Susan Abram, "Baseball Great Jackie Robinson Joined MLK at March on Washington," *Pasadena Star-News*, August 24, 2013.

"WE MARCH FOR INTEGRATED SCHOOLS NOW": NPR Staff, "A People's History of the March on Washington," *All Things Considered*, August 2, 2010, npr.org.

"I appeal to all of you": Lauren Feeney, "Two Versions of John Lewis's Speech," *Moyers and Company*, July 24, 2013, billmoyers.com.

"That was a real, real disappointment": Sondra Barrett Hassan, interviewed by Kelly Navies, October 9, 2013.

"any means necessary": "Malcolm X: 'By Any Means Necessary," video, *The Washington Post*, February 20, 2015, washingtonpost.com.

"I was afraid of him": Sondra Barrett Hassan, interviewed by Kelly Navies, October 9, 2013.

"He just knocked me out": Sondra Barrett Hassan, interviewed by Kelly Navies, October 9, 2013.

"I have a dream": Martin Luther King, Jr., "I Have a Dream," address delivered at the March on Washington for Jobs and Freedom, August 28, 1963, The Martin Luther King, Jr. Research and Education Institute, kinginstitutestanford.edu.

"Friends, at five o'clock": "Bayard Rustin Reads the Demands of the March," August 28, 1963, WGBH Media Library and Archives, Boston, MA, openvault.wgbh.org.

"It is now time for you to act": "Bayard Rustin Reads the Demands of the March," August 28, 1963, WGBH Media Library and Archives.

"The first demand": "Bayard Rustin Reads the Demands of the March," August 28, 1963, WGBH Media Library and Archives.

"He stood in the door": David Matthews, "Kennedy White House Had Jitters Ahead of 1963 March on Washington," CNN, August 28, 2013, cnn.com.

CHAPTER 6

"I learned that this was the way": Mary Beth Tinker, interviewed by Cayla Fox and Liz Groux, December 11, 2019, Washington, DC, Julian Bond History Project, directed by Greg Ivers, julianbondhistoryproject.org.

"We would come home": Susan Donaldson James, "Now Middle-Aged, Student Protesters Echo Triumphs and Casualties of the 1960s," *ABC News*, November 2, 2007, abcnews.go.com.

"STOP THE BOMBINGS": Max Frankel, "Demonstrators Decorous: 3 White House Aides Meet with Leaders," *The New York Times*, November 28, 1965.

"Freedom and destiny in America": Susan Dudley Gold, *Tinker v. Des Moines: Free Speech for Students* (Tarrytown, NY: Marshall Cavendish Benchmark, 2007), 14.

"I am the President": Frankel, "Demonstrators Decorous," November 28, 1965.

"The main impression": Gold, *Tinker v. Des Moines*, 14.

"The schools are no place": Jack Magarrell, "D.M. Schools Ban Wearing of Viet Truce Armbands," *Des Moines Register*, December 15, 1965.

"We talked to him about our conscience": Mary Beth Tinker, interviewed by Cayla Fox and Liz Groux, December 11, 2019.

"Well, I guess you're right": Mary Beth Tinker, interviewed by Cayla Fox and Liz Groux, December 11, 2019.

"I was very nervous": Mary Beth Tinker, interviewed by Cayla Fox and Liz Groux, December 11, 2019.

"Connie, I'm so sad": Mary Beth Tinker, interviewed by Cayla Fox and Liz Groux, December 11, 2019.

"She told me she was sorry": Doreen Rappaport, *Tinker vs. Des Moines: Student Rights on Trial* (New York: Harper Collins, 1993), 57.

"The counselor asked if I wanted": Joe Sergi, "Obscenity Case Files: *Tinker v. Des Moines Community School District*," Comic Book Legal Defense Fund, May 8, 2013, cbldf.org.

"I didn't want to wear it": "John Tinker on Protesting the Vietnam War in School," interview by C-SPAN, April 10, 2018, c-span.org.

"Are you sure you want to wear": Mike Kilen, "The Eccentric Life of the Former Des Moines Student Who Still Inspires Student Marches," *Des Moines Register*, March 22, 2018.

"Pinko! Commie!": Kilen, "The Eccentric Life," March 22, 2018.

"Look, you have your opinion": "John Tinker Describes the First Day Wearing a Black Armband to School to Protest the Vietnam War," Iowa Pathways, February 21, 2019, iowapbs.org.

"I suppose you know": Rappaport, *Tinker vs. Des Moines*, 41.

"In our system": *Tinker v. Des Moines Independent Community School District* 393 U.S. 503 (1969), law.cornell.edu.

"It can hardly be argued": *Tinker v. Des Moines Independent Community School District* 393 U.S. 503 (1969).

"My mom went and got some ice cream": Mary Beth Tinker, interviewed by Cayla Fox and Liz Groux, December 11, 2019.

"It was a terrible year for the war": Mary Beth Tinker, interviewed by Cayla Fox and Liz Groux, December 11, 2019.

CHAPTER 7

"You little Mexicans": *Taking Back the Schools*, episode 3, *Chicano! History of the Mexican-American Civil Rights Movement*, documentary, directed by Hector Galan, distributed by NLCC Educational Media, 1996.

"Oh, come on, Paula": Kyle Stokes, "50 Years Ago, Thousands Walked Out of East L.A. Schools. Now They Say 'The Fight Isn't Over,'" 89.3 KPCC, March 2, 2018, scpr .org.

"About 75 percent of the students": School statistics in this chapter are from Louis Sahagun, "East L.A., 1968: 'Walkout!' The Day High School Students Helped Ignite the Chicano Power Movement," *Los Angeles Times*, March 1, 2018.

"large dilapidated concrete buildings": Ian F. Haney Lopez, *Racism on Trial: The Chicano Fight for Justice* (Cambridge, MA: Belknap Press of Harvard University Press, 2003), 17.

"They patted us on the back": *Taking Back the Schools*, episode 3, *Chicano! History of the Mexican-American Civil Rights Movement*, 1996.

"Walkout! Walkout!": Sahagun, "East L.A., 1968: 'Walkout!' The Day High School Students Helped Ignite the Chicano Power Movement," March 1, 2018.

"You're free to go": Sahagun, "East L.A., 1968: 'Walkout!' The Day High School Students Helped Ignite the Chicano Power Movement," March 1, 2018.

"¡Viva la revolución!": Sahagun, "East L.A., 1968: 'Walkout!' The Day High School Students Helped Ignite the Chicano Power Movement," March 1, 2018.

"Walkout! Walkout!": Stokes, "50 Years Ago, Thousands Walked Out of East L.A. Schools. Now They Say 'The Fight Isn't Over,'" March 2, 2018.

"NO MORE FENCES": Rodolfo F. Acuña, *The Making of Chicana/o Studies: In the Trenches of Academe* (New Brunswick, NJ: Rutgers University Press, 2011), 41.

"WE ARE NOT 'DIRTY MEXICANS,'": Sign messages are drawn from various photographs and videos of the event. See also Sahagun, "East L.A., 1968: 'Walkout!' The Day High School Students Helped Ignite the Chicano Power Movement," March 1, 2018.

"absolutely tense": Mario T. Garcia and Sal Castro, *Blowout! Sal Castro and the Chicano Struggle for Educational Justice* (Chapel Hill, NC: University of North Carolina Press, 2011), 149.

"Man, we were scared": Louis Sahagun, "Thousands Honor '68 Walkouts by Mexican American Students," *Los Angeles Times*, March 9, 2008.

"But we were fed up": Sahagun, "Thousands Honor '68 Walkouts by Mexican American Students," March 9, 2008.

"I was scared, excited, nervous": *Latino Americans*, episode 5, *Prejudice and Pride*, documentary, produced by WETA Washington DC, Bosch and Co., Inc., Latino Public Broadcasting, in association with Independent Television Service, September 2013.

"What if I'm the only one": *Latino Americans*, episode 5, *Prejudice and Pride*, September 2013.

"**I was afraid to look behind**": *Latino Americans*, episode 5, *Prejudice and Pride*, September 2013.

"**Schools, not jails**": Miguel Roura, "Remembering the 1968 East Los Angeles High School Blowouts," *People's World*, May 11, 2018.

"**I felt like I was the grand marshal**": Garcia and Castro, *Blowout!* 173.

"**At that time, the boys**": Garcia and Castro, *Blowout!* 175.

"**We don't need the police**": Garcia and Castro, *Blowout!* 176.

"**He raised his fist**": Garcia and Castro, *Blowout!* 181.

"**I support fully**": Garcia and Castro, *Blowout!* 182.

"**We feel disturbed**": Garcia and Castro, *Blowout!* 186.

List of thirty-six demands: Garcia and Castro, *Blowout!* 186-187, and "The Walkout—How a Student Movement in 1968 Changed Schools Forever," February 26, 2018, unitedwayla.org.

"**I couldn't believe it**": Garcia and Castro, *Blowout!* 208.

CHAPTER 8

"**I am a 12-year-old girl**": Nessa Rabin, letter to President Ronald Reagan, no date [March 1981]. Rabin sent a copy of this letter to the editor of the *Barre-Montpelier Times Argus*, and the newspaper published it on March 27, 1981. *See* Children's Campaign for Nuclear Disarmament Records (CCNDR), 1980–1983, box 1, Swarthmore College Peace Collection, Swarthmore, Pennsylvania.

"**Thank you for your message**": Anne Higgins, letter to Nessa Rabin, May 4, 1981, CCNDR, box 1.

"**We keep in touch**": Neil Davis, "'Peace, Not Nuclear Weapons,' Children Say to Ronald Reagan," *Burlington Free Press*, June 21, 1981, newspaper clipping, CCNDR, box 1.

"**We were wondering**": Tom Slayton, "Wondering If They'll Be Alive in 20 Years Led Children on Campaign Against Nuclear Arms," *Vermont Life*, no date, newspaper clipping, CCNDR, box 1.

"**We had to get organized**": Davis, "'Peace, Not Nuclear Weapons,'" June 21, 1981.

"**We are children**": Children's Campaign for Nuclear Disarmament, untitled document, no date [Spring/Summer 1981], CCNDR, box 1.

"**We must stop this**": Sandra Gregor, "2 Temple Girls Push Reagan on Nukes," *Central Maine Morning Sentinel*, no date, newspaper clipping, CCNDR, box 1.

"**We received a lot of media coverage**": Monique Grodzki, letter to Nessa Rabin, June 20, 1981, CCNDR, box 3.

"**Kids can say things**": Slayton, "Wondering If They'll Be Alive in 20 Years Led Children on Campaign Against Nuclear Arms," no date.

"**If we get enough people**": Slayton, "Wondering If They'll Be Alive in 20 Years Led Children on Campaign Against Nuclear Arms," no date.

"**For all the kids**": Sarah Wilson, "Rally Draws 1,500 in Montpelier," *Barre-Montpelier Times Argus*, no date, newspaper clipping, CCNDR, box 1.

"**They are beautiful letters**": Children's Campaign for Nuclear Disarmament, letter to supporters, September 27, 1981, CCNDR, box 1.

"**a very bland letter**": Neil Davis, "Children to Visit D.C. with Anti-Nuke Letters," *Burlington Free Press*, October 6, 1981, newspaper clipping, CCNDR, box 1.

"**END THE NUCLEAR ARMS RACE**": These messages are taken from a photograph of the protesters on the day of the public reading and march, CCNDR, box 1.

"Dear President Reagan, I do not like war": "White House Office Snubs Vermont Girls' Campaign," *Sunday Times Argus*, October 18, 1981, newspaper clipping, CCNDR, box 1.

"really stupid . . . like two babies": "White House Office Snubs Vermont Girls' Campaign," *Sunday Times Argus*, October 18, 1981.

"No matter what country": "The Children's Campaign for Nuclear Disarmament," *The Children's Advocate*, no date, newspaper clipping, CCNDR, box 1.

"a big parade": William H. Braun, "No Easy Path to Mailroom at White House," *Burlington Free Press*, no date [October 1981], newspaper clipping, CCNDR, box 1.

"He's not President Reagan": Braun, "No Easy Path to Mailroom," no date [October 1981].

"The White House's refusal": "The Children's Campaign for Nuclear Disarmament," *The Children's Advocate*, no date.

"I'm sorry about the difficulties": Ronald Reagan, letter to Hannah Rabin and Friends, November 12, 1981, CCNDR, box 1.

"We appreciate the President's letter": Children's Campaign for Nuclear Disarmament, "Bulletin," no date [November 1981], CCNDR, box 1.

"It's depressing to go to Washington": Susan Buchsbaum, "The New Children's Crusade," no date [1982], newspaper clipping, CCNDR, box 1.

CHAPTER 9

"Hey, we've had some break-ins": A recording of this call is part of Seni Tienabeso, Matt Gutman, and Beth Lloyd, "George Zimmerman Jury Hears Key 911 Tapes in Start of Trial," *ABC News*, June 24, 2013, abcnews.go.com.

"something was off": Cara Buckley, "Jury Hears Zimmerman's Recorded Account of Night of Fatal Shooting," *The New York Times*, July 1, 2013.

"Did it ever occur to you": Buckley, "Jury Hears Zimmerman's Recorded Account of Night of Fatal Shooting," July 1, 2013.

"to investigate my son's murder": Tracy Martin and Sybrina Fulton, "Prosecute the Killer of Our Son, 17-Year-Old Trayvon Martin," no date [March 2012], change.org.

"I just want you to know": Tracy Martin, untitled speech, March 21, 2012, Union Square, New York City, "Tracy Martin & Sybrina Fulton Speak at Million Hoodies," posted March 23, 2012, youtube.com.

"Our son is your son": Sybrina Fulton, untitled speech, March 21, 2012, Union Square, New York City, "Tracy Martin & Sybrina Fulton Speak at Million Hoodies," posted March 23, 2012, youtube.com.

"SKITTLES + ICED TEA": Images of the signs and sounds of the chants are available at "Sights and Sounds of the Million Hoodie March," *TIME*, March 27, 2012, youtube.com.

"Justice for Trayvon": "Students at Two Miami-Dade Schools March for Trayvon," CBS Miami, March 22, 2012, miami.cbslocal.com.

"This is for you": Brian Hamacher, Ari Odzer, and Lisa Orkin Emmanuel, "Carol City High School Students Hold Trayvon Martin Walkout," NBC Miami, March 22, 2012, nbcmiami.com.

"Trayvon! Martin!": Hamacher, Odzer, and Emmanuel, "Carol City High," March 22, 2012.

"I can only imagine": Jackie Calmes and Helene Cooper, "A Personal Note as Obama Speaks on Death of Boy," *The New York Times*, March 23, 2012.

"It could have been me": "Students Across S. Fla. Walkout for Justice in Trayvon Martin Case," CBS Miami, March 23, 2012, Miami.cbslocal.com.

"What do we want": Auro Rojas, "Dr. Michael Krop High School Walkout/Protest for Trayvon Martin," March 23, 2012, youtube.com.

"This could be any one": "'Day of Unity' in Death of Trayvon Martin," CBS Miami, July 21, 2013, Miami.cbslocal.com.

"Before Trayvon, we took precautions": Channing Joseph and Ravi Somaiya, "Demonstrations Across Country Commemorate Trayvon Martin," *The New York Times*, July 20, 2013.

"Trayvon was a child": Joseph and Somaiya, "Demonstrations Across Country Commemorate Trayvon Martin," July 20, 2013.

"There's a new level of enthusiasm": Joseph and Somaiya, "Demonstrations Across Country Commemorate Trayvon Martin," July 20, 2013.

"love letter to Black people": Wesley Lowery, "Black Lives Matter: Birth of a Movement," *The Guardian*, January 17, 2017. This article includes the text of the letter cited in the chapter.

CHAPTER TEN

"My name is Anna Lee": Letter from Anna Lee Rain Yellowhammer to the US Army Corps of Engineers, *Treaties Still Matter: The Dakota Access Pipeline*, April 9, 2016, americanindian.si.edu. This is a copy of the original document, and it is the source for all of the chapter's quotations from the letter.

"Respect our water": Rezpect Our Water, "Rezpect Our Water," video, April 19, 2016, youtube.com.

"It's like they": Rezpect Our Water, "Rezpect Our Water: Sign Our Petition," video, April 27, 2016, youtube.com.

"In North Dakota alone": Letter from Run for Your Life Runners to Colonel John Henderson, US Army Corps of Engineers, May 3, 2016, indigenousrising.org.

"We are now taking": Ed Fallon, "Native Youth Runners Challenge President Obama," *Censored News*, no date, bsnorrell.blogspot.com.

"If I don't do it": Sisters Nation Color Guard, untitled post, March 18, 2017, facebook.com.

"We're sacrificing our bodies": Yessenia Funes, "'Divergent' Star Joins Native Youth Running to Protest Oil Pipeline," August 1, 2016, colorlines.com.

"We run!": For a version of this chant, see Rezpect Our Water, "We Run!" August 1, 2016, youtube.com.

"It brought some of the runners": See audio recording of Alice Brown Otter's comments embedded in "President Obama Dodges #NoDAPL Question as Native Youth Question His Commitment," September 8, 2016, indianz.com.

"All of a sudden": Evan Keeling, "Would You Run 2000 Miles to Stop the Dakota Access Pipeline?" no date, thenib.com.

"If the pipeline goes through": No name, "Tribe: Dakota Access Pipeline Threatens Water on Reservation," *Dayton Daily News*, August 12, 2016.

"It was an emotional meeting": Tariq Brownotter, "We Are Running for Our Lives," *MTV News*, August 1, 2016, mtv.com.

"Growing up on a Native American reservation": Brownotter, "We Are Running for Our Lives," August 1, 2016.

In response, the president told us": Brownotter, "We Are Running for Our Lives," August 1, 2016.

"Can't drink oil!": Dani Miller, "#NoDakotaAccess #NoDapl #RezpectOurWater," August 13, 2016, youtube.com.

"We run!" Miller, "#NoDakotaAccess," August 13, 2016.

"We knew that they were watching": No name, "President Obama Dodges #NoDAPL Question," September 8, 2016.

"All the youths": No name, "President Obama Dodges #NoDAPL Question," September 8, 2016.

"We just changed a lot of minds": No name, "President Obama Dodges #NoDAPL Question," September 8, 2016.

"water protectors": Allison Herrera, "Standing Rock Activists: Don't Call Us Protesters. We're Water Protectors," October 31, 2016, pri.org.

"We know he's listening": No name, "President Obama Dodges #NoDAPL Question," September 8, 2016.

"I'm willing to set my life": ABC News, "The Seventh Generation," documentary, 2017, abcnews.go.com.

"The best way to complete": Jack Healy and Nicholas Fandos, "Protesters Gain Victory in Fight Over Dakota Access Pipeline," *The New York Times*, December 4, 2016.

"I feel like I got": See video embedded in Naomi Klein, "The Lesson for Standing Rock: Organizing and Resistance Can Win," *The Nation*, December 4, 2016.

CHAPTER 11

"FEMINISM IS THE RADICAL NOTION": The sign messages in this chapter are drawn from numerous online photographs of the march.

"Who's the boss of girls": "List of Chants for Women's March 2017," no date, taskade.com. The text of these chants is also drawn from online videos of the march.

"likely the largest single day": Erica Chenoweth and Jeremy Pressman, "This Is What We Learned by Counting the Women's Marches," *The Washington Post*, February 7, 2017.

"Look at that face": Alan Rappeport, "Donald Trump's Uncomplimentary Comments About Carly Fiorina," *The New York Times*, September 10, 2015.

"fat pigs, dogs, slobs": Aaron Blake, "Here Are the Megyn Kelly Questions That Donald Trump Is Still Sore About," *The Washington Post*, January 26, 2016.

"We believe that women's rights": Women's March, "Unity Principles," no date, womensmarch.com.

"support and solidarity": Homepage, *Pussyhat Project: Design Interventions for Social Change*, no date, pussyhatproject.com.

"My sisters and siblings are being beaten": "Voices of the Women's March: Angela Davis, Gloria Steinem, Madonna, Alicia Keys, Janet Mock & More," *Democracy Now*, January 23, 2017, democracynow.org.

"Pope Francis, I want to tell you": Lauren Gambino, "Francis and Sophie's Secret: Girl Who Hugged Pope Delivers Immigration Plea," *The Guardian*, September 23, 2015.

"Her mind is very powerful": Hernandez, "The Girl Who Hugged the Pope Is at the White House," May 5, 2016.

"Hi, everybody": For footage of all speeches, including Cruz's, see "Women's March on Washington," C-SPAN, January 21, 2017, c-span.org.

"**because I am a girl**": Lillian Martosko, "The Women's March on Washington," *Scholastic Kids Press*, January 23, 2017, kpcnotebook.scholastic.com.

CHAPTER 12

"**At around 2:30, we heard**": "Video: Student David Hogg During Florida School Shooting: 'It's Time to Take a Stand' on Gun Control," *Los Angeles Times*, February 15, 2018.

"**I personally have rallied**": "Video: Student David Hogg During Florida School Shooting: 'It's Time to Take a Stand' on Gun Control," February 15, 2018.

"**I call on the legislators**": Video: Student David Hogg During Florida School Shooting: 'It's Time to Take a Stand' on Gun Control," February 15, 2018.

"**Contact your state and local**": Founders, *Glimmer of Hope*, 71-72.

"**no more guns**": Julie Turkewitz, Patricia Mazzei, and Audra D.S. Burch, "'How Did This Happen?' Grief and Fury after Florida Shooting," *The New York Times*, February 16, 2018. See the video that accompanies this news article.

"**Stay alert. #Never Again**": Emily Witt, "How the Survivors of Parkland Began the Never Again Movement," *The New Yorker*, February 19, 2018.

"**He didn't even mention**": Matt Pierce, Jennie Jarvie, Molly Hennessy-Fiske, "Horrified Florida Students Beg the Adults: Please, Do Something About Guns," *Los Angeles Times*, February 16, 2018.

"**We certainly do not understand**": CNN Staff, "Florida Student Emma González to Lawmakers and Gun Advocates: 'We Call BS,'" CNN, February 17, 2018, cnn.com.

"**Throw them out**": CNN Staff, "Florida Student Emma González to Lawmakers and Gun Advocates: 'We Call BS,' " February 17, 2018.

"**People are saying**": Quinn Scanlon, "Florida Teen Shooting Survivors Announce 'March for Our Lives' Demonstration in Washington," *ABC News*, February 18, 2018, abcnews.go.com.

"**Students all over the country**": "Transcript: Florida School Shooting Survivors on 'Face the Nation,' February 18, 2018," cbsnews.com.

"**Not one more**": The entire statement quoted here no longer appears at marchforourlives.com. But it is accessible on Pinterest; the Facebook page of March for Our Lives, Fort Worth, Texas; and other online sites that archived the statement.

"**President Trump, you control**": "Transcript: Florida School Shooting Survivors on 'Face the Nation,' February 18, 2018," cbsnews.com.

"**That's infuriating**": Julie Turkewitz and Vivian Yee, "With Grief and Hope, Florida Students Take Gun Control Fight on the Road," *The New York Times*, February 20, 2018.

"**We can't stop the crazies**": Julie Turkewitz, "Florida Students Began with Optimism. Then They Spoke to Lawmakers," *The New York Times*, February 21, 2018.

"**I just want to know why**": Turkewitz, "Florida Students Began with Optimism," February 21, 2018.

"**I think that if you look**": Turkewitz, "Florida Students Began with Optimism," February 21, 2018.

"**Shame! Shame! Shame!**": Turkewitz, "Florida Students Began with Optimism," February 21, 2018.

"**So, Senator Rubio, can you tell me**": Emanuella Grinberg, "Students at Town Hall to Washington, NRA: Guns Are the Problem, Do Something," CNN, February 22, 2018, cnn.com. Accompanying this article is a series of videos of the town hall. Quotations are drawn from the article and the videos.

"In the name of seventeen people": Grinberg, "Students at Town Hall," February 22, 2018.

"Would you agree": Grinberg, "Students at Town Hall," February 22, 2018.

"reconsidering": Grinberg, "Students at Town Hall," February 22, 2018.

"You made your voices heard": Jenny Jarvie, "Bucking the NRA, Florida Governor Signs Landmark Gun Control Legislation," *Los Angeles Times*, March 9, 2018.

"not perfect": Patricia Mazzei, "Florida Governor Signs Gun Limits into Law, Breaking with the N.R.A.," *The New York Times*, March 9, 2018.

"We want change": Joe Heim, Marissa J. Lange, and Susan Svruluga, "Thousands of Students Walk Out of School in Nationwide Gun Violence Protest," *The Washington Post*, March 14, 2018. This news article, like many articles about the walkout, includes a video of the protest.

"We should never go": John Bacon and Christal Hayes, "'We Deserve Better': Students Nationwide Walk Out in Massive Protest Over Gun Violence," *USA Today*, March 14, 2018.

"To the parents supporting their children": Bacon and Hayes, "'We Deserve Better': Students Nationwide Walk Out in Massive Protest Over Gun Violence," March 14, 2018.

"To be honest, I'm scared": Peter Jamison, Joe Heim, Lori Aratani, and Marissa J. Lange, "'Never Again!' Students Demand Action Against Gun Violence in Nation's Capital," *The Washington Post*, March 24, 2018.

"It was a never-ending stream": Founders, *Glimmer of Hope*, 149.

"blown away": Founders, *Glimmer of Hope*, 154.

"Who are we? MSD!": Founders, *Glimmer of Hope*, 158.

"To the leaders, skeptics, and cynics": Quotations from speakers and performers at the march are drawn from "March for Our Lives Rally," C-Span, March 24, 2018, c-span.org.

"freaking out inside": Founders, *Glimmer of Hope*, 162.

"WHAT DO YOU LIKE MORE": Sign messages are drawn from numerous online photographs and videos of the march.

"I have a dream": Nick Penzenstadler, "March for Our Lives: Martin Luther King Jr.'s Granddaughter Has Dream 'Enough Is Enough,'" *USA Today*, March 24, 2018.

"We believe in the Second Amendment": "March for Our Lives Highlights: Students Protesting Guns Say 'Enough Is Enough,'" *The New York Times*, March 24, 2018.

"a year of unparalleled success": Matt Vasilogambros, "After Parkland, States Pass 50 New Gun-Control Laws," Pew Charitable Trusts, August 2, 2018, pewtrusts.org.

CHAPTER 13

"That was very scary for me": "'Why Go to School When You Have No Future?' A Q&A With a 13-Year-Old Climate Striker," *The Nation*, March 14, 2019.

"My chest started to get prickly": Carolyn Kormann, "New York's Original Teen-Age Climate Striker Welcomes a Global Movement," *The New Yorker*, September 21, 2019.

"She was really upset": Kormann, "New York's Original Teen-Age Climate Striker Welcomes a Global Movement," September 21, 2019.

"I started to really research": Aria Bendix, "Greta Thunberg Isn't the Only Climate Activist You Should Know," *Business Insider*, December 7, 2019.

"My classmates were concerned": Jonathan Watts, "Greta Thunberg, Schoolgirl Climate Change Warrior," *The Guardian*, March 11, 2019.

"I kept that to myself": Watts, "Greta Thunberg, Schoolgirl Climate Change Warrior," March 11, 2019.

"sometimes a bit different": Alison Rourke, "Greta Thunberg Responds to Asperger's Critics: 'It's a Superpower,' " *The Guardian*, September 2, 2019.

"I told them about my worries": Watts, "Greta Thunberg, Schoolgirl Climate Change Warrior," March 11, 2019.

"That's when I kind of realized": Watts, "Greta Thunberg, Schoolgirl Climate Change Warrior," March 11, 2019.

"When school started in August": Greta Thunberg, "I'm Striking from School to Protest Inaction on Climate Change—You Should Too," *The Guardian*, November 26, 2018.

"SKOLSTEJK FOR KLIMATET": Thunberg, "I'm Striking from School to Protest Inaction on Climate Change—You Should Too," (photo), November 26, 2018.

"I tried to bring people along": Kate Aronoff, "How Greta Thunberg's Lone Strike Against Climate Change Became a Global Movement," *Rolling Stone*, March 5, 2019.

"I've learned that you are never": Greta Thunberg, "Greta Thunberg Addressed the COP24 Plenary Session," December 12, 2018, fridaysforfuture.org. Videos and transcripts of Thunberg's major speeches are accessible at fridaysforfuture.org.

"You are not mature enough": Thunberg, "Greta Thunberg Addressed the COP24 Plenary Session," December 12, 2018.

"You say you love": Thunberg, "Greta Thunberg Addressed the COP24 Plenary Session," December 12, 2018.

"We have not come here": Thunberg, "Greta Thunberg Addressed the COP24 Plenary Session," December 12, 2018.

"She just put them in their place": Sarah Kaplan, "How a 7th-Grader's Strike Against Climate Change Exploded into a Movement," *The Washington Post*, February 16, 2019.

"SCHOOL STRIKE 4 CLIMATE": See photo accompanying Kaplan, "How a 7th-Grader's Strike Against Climate Change Exploded into a Movement," February 16, 2019.

"Like Greta says, if people": Lucy Diavolo, "Meet Alexandria Villaseñor, the Teen Activist Who's Spent 12 Fridays Outside the United Nations Striking for the Climate," *Teen Vogue*, March 1, 2019.

"I chose the United Nations": "14-Year-Old Alexandria Villaseñor Has Been Striking Outside UN Headquarters for 5 Months. Here's Why," Earthrise, May 23, 2019, earthday.org.

"she got mad": Kormann, "New York's Original Teen-Age Climate Striker Welcomes a Global Movement," September 21, 2019.

"They understand my point of view": "Kids Lead Protests to Fight Climate Change," CBS News, February 22, 2019, cbsnews.com.

"The idea is to collectively fight": Rose Minutaglio, "The World Is Burning. These Girls Are Fighting to Save It," *Elle*, March 14, 2019, elle.com.

"I hope there are policies": " 'Why Go to School When You Have No Future?' A Q&A With a 13-Year-Old Climate Striker," *The Nation*, March 14, 2019.

"To those of you who deny the truth": See online videos, especially Twitter feeds, of the March 15 school strike in New York City.

"Well, Mummy just has the news on": Jake Offenhartz, "Liveblog: Students Go on Strike to Demand Action on Climate Change," *Gothamist*, March 15, 2019, gothamist.com.

"DENIAL IS NOT A POLICY": Sign messages and chants are drawn from online photographs and videos of the March 15 protest.

"Money won't matter": Jake Offenhartz, "Liveblog: Students Go on Strike to Demand Action on Climate Change," March 15, 2019.

"fossils": Catherine Gioino and Ben Chapman, "Students Strike for Climate Change in New York City—and Around the World," *New York Daily News*, March 15, 2019.

"11 minutes of silence": Alexandria Villaseñor, untitled post, May 24, 2019, twitter.com.

"Earth Uprising's main goal": "14-Year-Old Alexandria Villaseñor Has Been Striking Outside UN Headquarters for 5 Months. Here's Why," Earthrise, May 23, 2019, earthday.org.

"We feel a lot of adults": Greta Thunberg and 46 Youth Activists, "Young People Have Led the Climate Strike. Now We Need Adults to Join Us Too," *The Guardian*, May 23, 2019.

"But to change everything": Thunberg and 46 Youth Activists, "Young People Have Led the Climate Strike. Now We Need Adults to Join Us Too," May 23, 2019.

"I know there are people": Jake Offenhartz, "Updates: NYC Students Go on Strike to Demand Action on Climate Crisis," *Gothamist*, September 20, 2019.

"A better world is possible": Chants are drawn from online interviews of those who marched from Foley Square to Battery Park, September 20, 2019.

"A lot of us are giving up": Madeline Carlisle, "'This Is an Emergency. Our House Is on Fire.' Greta Thunberg Addresses New York's Climate Strike," *TIME*, September 20, 2019.

"Hi, everyone!": "Climate Strike in New York City," Move On, September 20, 2019, youtube.com. All Villaseñor quotations in this section are drawn from this source.

"Hello, New York City": "Climate Strike in New York City," Move On, September 20, 2019, youtube.com. All Thunberg quotations here, plus those of the crowd, are drawn from this source.

"The United States, having vowed": Somini Sengupta and Lisa Friedman, "At U.N. Climate Summit, Few Commitments and US Silence," *The New York Times*, September 23, 2019.

CHAPTER 14

"UNSTOPPABLE, UNDENIABLE": "Students March for DREAMers in Washington, DC," *NowThis News*, November 8, 2019, youtube.com.

"People are just breaking down": Julie Preston and John H. Cushman, Jr., "Obama to Permit Young Migrants to Remain in U.S.," *The New York Times*, June 15, 2012.

"I hereby pledge": United We Dream, "Day 2: UWD Citizenship Ceremony," July 10, 2013, youtube.com.

"I am so fed up": United We Dream, "DREAMers Stop Deportation Bus in Ongoing Escalation at ICE Facility in Phoenix," August 22, 2013, unitedwedream.org.

"RESIST DEPORTATIONS": Sign messages and chants are drawn from "Students March for DREAMers in Washington, DC," *NowThis News*, November 8, 2019.

"I'm here today": This quotation, as well as all remaining quotes in the chapter, are drawn from "Students March for DREAMers in Washington, DC," *NowThis News*, November 8, 2019.

"I've been on the edge": See video in Pete Williams and Adam Edelman, "Supreme Court Blocks Trump from Ending DACA in Big Win for Dreamers," June 18, 2020, *NBC News*.

CHAPTER 15

"As a Black girl": The Learning Network, "What Students Are Saying About the George Floyd Protests," *The New York Times*, June 4, 2020.

"I can't breathe": Richard A. Oppel, Jr. and Kim Barker, "New Transcripts Detail Last Moments for George Floyd," *The New York Times*, July 8, 2020.

"Black Lives Matter!": Patricia Sullivan and others, "Thousands Gathered Across City to Protest Death of George Floyd," *The Washington Post*, June 7, 2020.

"We should do something": Miranda Bryant, "'It Was Time to Take Charge': The Black Youth Leading the George Floyd Protests," *The Guardian*, June 15, 2020.

"We are standing in solidarity": Aryia Dattamajumdar and Victoria Stafford, "Berkeley High School Students Bring Awareness to Black Lives Matter, School Segregation," *Daily Californian*, June 7, 2020.

"Teachers need to be taught": Dattamajumdar and Stafford, "Berkeley High School Students," June 7, 2020.

"We need young children": Dattamajumdar and Stafford, "Berkeley High School Students," June 7, 2020.

"Berkeley High School Students are organizing": "Berkeley High School Students Call to Protest: Stand with Black Youth," posted by East Bay Democratic Socialists of America, June 8, 2020, facebook.com.

"This isn't just Black kids": George Kelly, "Berkeley High Protest Takes Aim at Racism in Justice, Education Systems," *Mercury News*, June 9, 2020.

"BLACK LIVES MATTER; STAND WITH BLACK YOUTH": For all cited truck signs, see videos posted by Ray Chavez and George Kelly in Kelly, "Berkeley High Protest Takes Aim," June 9, 2020.

"We're really trying": Kelly, "Berkeley High Protest Takes Aim," June 9, 2020.

"We are lifting up the Black youth": For these and subsequent comments made by the march's organizers, as well as chants by the marchers, see videos posted by @allaboutgeorge, June 9, 2020, twitter.com. Some of these videos are embedded in Kelly, "Berkeley High Protest Takes Aim," June 9, 2020.

"SOLIDARITY FROM THE BAY": See photos and videos at Tracey Taylor, "Black Lives Matter March Run by BHS Students Ends with Street Painting," *Berkeleyside*, June 9, 2020.

"I CAN'T BREATHE": See photos at Kelly, "Berkeley High Protest Takes Aim," June 9, 2020.

Photo Credits